THE LIFE OF WALTER PATER

WALTER PATER.

FROM "OXFORD CHARACTERS," BY W. ROTHENSTEIN.

Lent by Mr. John Lane, publisher of "Oxford Characters."

THE LIFE OF
WALTER PATER

BY

THOMAS WRIGHT

AUTHOR OF "THE LIFE OF EDWARD FITZGERALD,"
"THE LIFE OF SIR RICHARD BURTON," ETC.

WITH SEVENTY-EIGHT PLATES

TWO VOLUMES

VOL. I

HASKELL HOUSE PUBLISHERS Ltd.
Publishers of Scarce Scholarly Books
NEW YORK, N. Y. 10012
1969

WHITTEMORE LIBRARY
Framingham State College
Framingham, Massachusetts

First Published **1907**

HASKELL HOUSE PUBLISHERS LTD.
Publishers of Scarce Scholarly Books
280 LAFAYETTE STREET
NEW YORK, N. Y. 10012

Library of Congress Catalog Card Number: **68-24928**

Standard Book Number 8383-0178-9

Printed in the United States of America

This Work is
Dedicated,
by kind permission,
to the
Rev. Arthur J. Galpin, M.A.,
Head Master of
Walter Pater's School,
The King's School, Canterbury.

INSCRIPTION [1]

For Y^e Life of Walter Pater
To Y^e Reader

Reader! I in this book implanted have,
  As in a pleasaunce, thoughts which be ye floweres;
Sore blasts of critiques keen they may ne brave
  And sure would die ybent with envious showeres
Howbeit, here's a fragrant rose or two
  Of pious musings; and some rosemarie,—
That aunciant mem'ries—and a little rue
  Of things more sombre; weedes ne doubt there be
  The which yourselves must delve and grubbe up carefullie.

Scorn not my booke, whate'er it be
Good Reader in thy courtesie;
If I speke truth, your laudès do not grudge,
If I speke false, my righteous God will judge.

---

(1) These pleasant lines, from some old English author whose name we have not been able to trace, were inserted by Walter Pater in front of a book of manuscript poems commenced in March, 1859, and bore as title

INSCRIPTION
FOR Y^E POET'S BOOKE
TO Y^E READER.

PREFACE.

It is now more than twelve years since Walter Pater died, but although he was one of the most brilliant and most original writers of the Victorian era no account of his life has yet appeared, with the exception of the meagre outline given in Mr. A. C. Benson's *Walter Pater,* and the few details to be found in scattered magazine articles. Moreover, amazing to say, slight as are these various accounts, and although they are understood to have been inspired by some of Pater's relatives, they are crowded with the most astonishing, the most staggering errors. To point out all these errors would only make the reader weary, so I will confine myself for the present solely to Mr. Benson's little book. Against Mr. Benson personally, let it be at once said, I certainly have no animus. We are well known to each other by correspondence. He has always written to me with the courtesy of an English gentleman, and I hope I have never in my replies allowed myself to be outdone under this head. Soon after my *Life of Edward FitzGerald* appeared I had the pleasure of complying with his request that he might make use of certain portions for his monograph in "The English Men of Letters Series"; and I feel sure that if I should ever require any assistance from him he would cheerfully do anything for me in his power. Let me also express the hope that his work which—all said and done—is chiefly a book of criticism, will, after the revision which it so much needs, go into many editions—for it is quite impossible in this slap-dash and slip-shod age to have too much of and about the careful and scrupulously conscientious Walter Pater, and I may add, of the judicious criticism of Mr. Benson.

Mr. Benson's principal errors of commission and omission are as follows:—

(1) He makes the astounding statement (p. 210) that Pater "did not arrive at his plentiful vocabulary as some writers have done by the production of large masses of writing that never see the light," and on page 209 he says, "It is a curious fact that Pater showed no precocious signs in boyhood and youth of a desire to write. . . Pater's family cannot remember that he ever showed any particular tendency to write." That is to say, Pater the author sprang into being like a phœnix. As a matter of fact, both as a boy and as a young man he wrote enormously. He was, as these pages will show, perhaps the most voluminous boy-author who ever lived.

(2) Mr. Benson says (p. 209) Pater "never wrote poetry in childhood except a few humorous verses." On the contrary he wrote thousands of lines of serious poetry. I have in my own possession many hundreds of them, and I have been promised more.

(3) He states that Roman Catholicism in the Pater family was of late date. On the contrary the Paters are a very old Catholic family.

(4) He does not once mention Harbledown where Pater lived all the time he attended the King's School at Canterbury.

(5) He says (p. 3) that Pater was popular at school. On the contrary, as these pages will show, no boy could possibly have been more unpopular there.

(6) He says that Pater was apt to be reticent about his own interior feelings. On the contrary, when with very intimate friends like McQueen and Richard C. Jackson, he wore his heart on his sleeve. He told them everything. Had it not been so this book would have been sadly lacking in details.

(7) Mr. Benson does not once mention five of Pater's most intimate friends, Dombrain, McQueen, Richard C. Jackson, Richard Robinson, and M. B. Moorhouse;

and this is the more remarkable because the first three were almost daily in his company for four, five, and seventeen years respectively, and shared all his confidences. No friendships, as these pages will show, could possibly have been more intimate or more interesting. To omit Mr. Jackson is to tell the story of David and leave out Jonathan.

(8) Mr. Benson tells nothing about the great central event of Pater's life—his connection with the St. Austin's "Monkery," which is something like giving an account of Wellington and leaving out the Peninsular War and Waterloo.

(9) He says (p. 11), that Pater's chief interest in his early life was philosophy. It was not so. His chief interest during all his youth and early manhood was English Literature.

(10) He says (p. 13)—and perhaps this is the most amazing error of all—that Pater's metaphysical studies did not destroy his strong religious instinct. On the contrary, as Mr. Gosse (*Critical Kit-Kats,* p. 250) says, and as our own pages prove, Pater was for many years quite severed from religion. He had his period of active revolt, as had John Bunyan and John Newton.

(11) He gives scarcely any anecdotes about Pater, and records only two or three uninteresting conversations.

(12) He says (p. 185) that Pater "wrote very few letters"—a legend to be found in most accounts of Pater, who, on the contrary, wrote an enormous number of letters—as many as four hundred, indeed, to one friend—and most of them long letters.

I am also sorry to notice that Mr. Benson tries to justify Pater at the expense of Jowett. But, at the period to which we refer, Pater was hopelessly in the wrong, and the attitude that Jowett assumed and the action that he took were such as all men acquainted with the whole story must unhesitatingly approve (see

Chapter 29). In short, although Pater had many admirable qualities, and many graces to which we shall endeavour to do justice, he was neither a saint nor a martyr.

But to the ordinary reader the most amazing fact in connection with Mr. Benson's book is the announcement in his preface that he had "the most kind and courteous assistance throughout" from some of Pater's closest friends. We are quite sure that these friends did not wittingly mislead Mr. Benson, and equally sure that Mr. Benson put down nothing which he believed to be incorrect. What then, it will be asked, is the explanation? The answer is a simple one. Pater had a curious dislike to mingling his friendships, and a persistent habit of concealing from one friend what he would reveal to another. For example, I discovered that Mr. Richard C. Jackson, a friend, as we said, of seventeen years' standing, had never heard of Mr. Moorhouse, and I do not suppose that Mr. Moorhouse ever heard of Mr. Jackson, while neither of them is once mentioned in Mr. Benson's pages. Mr. Jackson, Mr. Gosse, Dr. Shadwell, Mr. Richard Robinson, and Dr. Lee were all friends of Pater—but, having little in common with one another, they rarely met, and Pater scarcely ever spoke to one about the others. Thus it is not at all surprising that those from whom Mr. Benson derived his knowledge made amazing mistakes, or that they were absolutely ignorant of what we shall prove to have been the salient events of Pater's life. The condition of affairs then is owing not to them but to the peculiarity of Pater's temperament—and very peculiar it must have been if (and Mr. Benson says it was so) persons could live with him twenty years, during which he wrote tens of thousands of lines of both prose and poetry, and not be aware that he was a writer at all.

In any circumstances, and from whatever causes, the public have been supplied with a vast number of statements, by various writers, about Pater, which I shall show to be absolutely fictitious, and this alone would be sufficient justification for the present work—although to correct the errors of predecessors is but a small portion of my self-imposed task.

The work was commenced about four years ago, and would have appeared as early as 1905 but for an event in the publishing world to which there is no need to make further reference. Residing in Olney and within walking distance of Weston Underwood, the old home of the Paters, and having long been on terms of intimacy with a number of members of the Pater family, it is not surprising that, my *Life of Edward FitzGerald* finished, I should set myself to write on Pater. The connection of the Pater family with the Poet Cowper and the yarns which I had often heard from the lips of old inhabitants of Olney and Weston also had their influence over me.

From what has already been said the reader will have judged—and correctly—that nearly the whole of this work is new. It is the kind of work, too (if I may without egotism say so), in which Pater himself would have gloried. Previous writers on the subject have been satisfied with generalising—and with generalising from details that were insufficient or false. Pater utterly detested this kind of thing. He was never tired of girding at the eighteenth century with its dislike of detail, and he shows in his Preface to Dr. Shadwell's edition of the *Purgatorio*, that it was this characteristic —this hatred of a circumstantial account of anything— which blinded that century to the virtues of Dante.[1] The minuteness of Dante's handiwork, he tells us—his care for elaboration of detail—repelled our forefathers as much as it attracts us. To be sealed of the tribe of Dante then—especially as Pater himself was of that tribe sealed—is only what the public have a right to expect of a biographer of Pater. Of the events that

---

(1) See Chapter xliii., § 170.

are dealt with in the first seventeen chapters of this book absolutely nothing has previously been recorded beyond what might be put in half-a-dozen lines. "I am very glad," said Mr. Edmund Gosse to me, "that you intend giving so full an account of Pater's early life (1839 to 1859), for of that hardly anything is known."

On Pater's ancestry and the connection of the family with Weston Underwood and Olney I have been able to throw much new light, my information being derived from the Catholic registers at Olney, which were kindly examined for me by the Rev. F. Carton de Wiart, and from several members of the Pater family, including Mr. John E. Pater of Olney. For the extracts from the Thornton Registers I have to thank Dr. Bradbrook of Bletchley.

Of Pater's childhood at Enfield and Tonbridge a full account is given, my informants and helpers being Mr. John James Pater, Mr. Edgar Aloysius Pater, Mrs. Goodwin (Mira Pater), Mrs. Comber (Eleanor Pater), and Mr. John Fagg.

My pages will be found particularly rich in reminiscences of Walter Pater's "saintly boyhood" at Canterbury, and I have to thank for much kind assistance in connection with this period the Right Rev. Bishop Mitchinson, formerly Head-Master of the King's School; the Rev. A. J. Galpin, the present Head-Master, to whom this book is, by permission, dedicated; the Rev. J. B. Kearney, who figures conspicuously in these pages; and the following old King's School boys—Mr. George Spain,[1] the Rev. Dr. Chafy, the Rev. Henry Biron, Sir George Collard, and Mr. J. R. McQueen.

My pen quite fails me in my endeavours to express my gratitude to Mr. McQueen for his countless favours. But for him this book would have had a huge and unseemly gap. Indeed in the whole course of my

---

[1] It is also interesting to note that Mr. Spain's sister married one of the sons of Mr. Anby Beatson, the Second Master of the King's School.

literary career I have never met with a more courteous and generous helper. He has taken the trouble to write scores of letters, and he has patiently answered to the best of his ability hundreds of questions, by word of mouth as well as by letter, for I have several times had the pleasure of being his guest at Chailey. I have also been much helped by the manuscript notes made by Mr. McQueen in a copy of Mr. Benson's book and in a copy of the work on Pater written by Mr. Ferris Greenslet. The latter book, although it contains a few apposite observations, is a most lamentable performance. As an example, and a fair example of Mr. Greenslet's style, I may give one little remark of his on Pater's study "Diaphanéité." He says, "The whole composition moves with unwonted resiliency and speed"—which is absurd enough when one remembers that "resiliency" is the quality of leaping back. "I observed the 'resiliency'," comments Mr. McQueen, "but I am never surprised at anything I read in these little memoirs about Pater. The authors seem to think fine writing makes up for ignorance of facts." [1]

It had not previously been known that Pater wrote anything before 1863, but I am able, as I have already intimated, to prove that he was one of the most prolific of schoolboy writers, and that in his undergraduate days he was equally industrious with his pen. Of the poems written by him at this period, a number, some of them long poems and signed, have been placed in my hands, but I have not printed them in this book, for, although (owing to their wealth of biographical detail) they have been of enormous service to me in the writing of it, they are by no means masterpieces. They are pretty, that is all; and such being the case, and taking into consideration the reception of the *Essays from the Guardian,* when issued in book-form, I have judged that lovers of Pater would resent their appearance at the present moment. I have,

---

[1] Letter to me, 10th April, 1905.

however, given a sufficient account of them, with here and there a line of quotation.

My sketch of the Queen's College period is enriched with a number of curious details, and enlivened by amusing anecdotes—my chief helpers having been the Rev. Canon Capes (Pater's Tutor), the Right Rev. Bishop Mitchinson (Master of Pembroke College, Oxford), Professor Bywater, the Rev. M. B. Moorhouse, and the Rev. Oswald Reichel.

Lastly, there is the long Brasenose period, and in writing it I was assisted by a friend indeed—none other, in fact, than Mr. Richard C. Jackson, the original of Marius the Epicurean. Mr. Jackson has helped me in a hundred ways, and I have spent many agreeable hours with him, both at his house in Camberwell and in mine at Olney. That Mr. Jackson was the original of Marius, Pater was often heard to say; and a circumstantial account of the long and intimate friendship that subsisted between him and Mr. Jackson, and of Pater's connection with the St. Austin's "Monkery"— the central event of his life, though not one word about it can be found elsewhere—will also be given. No other writer on Pater, indeed, seems ever to have heard of Mr. Jackson or of the remarkable St. Austin's episode. This portion of my book overflows with anecdotes and interesting and inspiring conversations between Pater and his various friends. I also recall the kindness of Mr. Edmund Gosse who, to use an expression in one of his letters, gave me his "best memories" of Walter Pater. The Rev. Dr. Bussell made me his debtor by answering a number of questions during an interview which I had with him at Brasenose, by the gift of a copy of his sermon on Pater, and by sending me the entries concerning Pater in the Brasenose books. Dr. Shadwell's prefaces to Pater's works, the introductions to his edition of Dante's *Purgatorio*, and his useful, though very imperfect, Bibliography [1] of

---

[1] A complete Bibliography of Pater will be found in our Appendix

Pater at the beginning of *Miscellaneous Studies*, have been of considerable assistance to me; and I have also to acknowledge my indebtedness to Pater's colleagues —the Rev. Dr. Hornby, Provost of Eton, and the Rev. Canon Shand; and to Pater's pupils, the Rev. Oswald Birchall, the Rev. Anthony Bathe, the Rev. Alfred Bedson, and the Rev. T. W. Adam. The late Mr. William Sharp assisted me over and over again, answered many questions and was kind enough to send me the excellent portrait of him which we are able to reproduce; Mr. John Payne has rendered me various most acceptable services; and I owe a few facts to Mr. John Churton Collins, who communicated them during a delightful walk together (on the 24th of August, 1906), to Cowper's woodland haunts and the house of the Paters at Weston. The assistance I received from Mr. Watts-Dunton, who kindly looked over a few of the chapters for me, and from Mr. A. C. Swinburne, with whom I had the pleasure of an interview, was mainly of a negative character. It has been assumed by several previous writers that Pater was intimately acquainted with Mr. Swinburne and D. G. Rossetti, but this is a mistake. I have Mr. Watts-Dunton's authority for saying that Rossetti "did not know Pater at all, save that he once saw him for five minutes in his studio," and Mr. Swinburne told me that he never met Pater, to speak to him, more than twice—once in London and once at Oxford, and that even then only a few words passed.

I have spared no pains to be accurate, and my investigations have obliged me to contradict flatly (though I hope courteously) much that has been written about Pater by superficial or less privileged writers. I have written in support of no theory, but although I feel for Pater a sympathy bordering on love I have not attempted to conceal from myself and others his grave faults, which, however, I have tried to show, were in some degree attributable to the society into which he was thrown. In short my ambition is that the critics and the public should say of this book—"It tells the truth, though only just as much as the public has a right to know, and tells it in the most delicate manner conceivable." In spite of occasional appearances to the contrary, the careful student of Pater's life will observe, as did Lady Dilke, a gradual ennobling of Pater's character until at last he is seen to have regained the faith and the scrupulous rectitude of his boyhood. Indeed, the reader may, if so disposed, and in accordance with a suggestion already made, regard him as an æsthetic—a High Church—John Bunyan or John Newton—men who in their latter days looked back with distress on an unsatisfactory past; dwellers in Mesech who eventually worked their way into a more satisfying country.

As previous writers have assumed that Pater was a great authority on Greek Art and the Renaissance period, the conclusion I have been forced to come to in respect to Pater's scholarship will necessarily give most readers something of a shock. I refer to my remarks at the end of Chapters 28 and 39, in which I have pointed out (and my knowledge has been derived not only from the study of Pater's works but also from the admissions of some of his nearest friends) that Pater's knowledge, even of the subjects with which he was supposed to be most intimate, was by no means deep. He glowed with genuine love for delicate perfection, but he was too indolent to turn up his sleeves, as it were, and apply himself to the tremendous work of getting to the foundation of things. The truth is that for his own peculiar art he did not require a prodigious amount of knowledge. He is the grasshopper of English literature. "Thou sippest a little dew," we may say to him, and

"Straight thou makest the woods and hills
Echo all with thy dulcet trills."(1)

(1) "The Grasshopper," by Remy Belleau. Translated by Mr. John Payne in Section II. ("The Renaissance,") of his *Flowers of France.*

And, after all, intuition is everything. There is more Greek feeling in Pater even than in Landor, who was a profound scholar as well as a great writer; there is more Greek feeling in Pater, indeed, than in any other English litterateur, with the exception of Keats.

In writing this book I have endeavoured to bear in mind that the first duty of a biographer is to try to avoid hurting the feelings of any living person. With this in view I have gone through my manuscript again and again, and have struck out everything that seemed likely to give offence. Thus I have thought it well to omit all Pater's jibes at religion. As regards the Jowett incident, I have given Pater's antagonist his precise due. Because I am writing the Life of Pater that is no reason why I should blacken the memory of every man who could not see eye to eye with him. However, with my treatment of this incident, and of some others which are also delicate in the extreme, I feel sure the most captious will find no fault. Pater's home life—his life with his sisters—I have considered absolutely sacred, and there will be found in these pages nothing whatever about it—that is to say, nothing subsequent to his childhood; and, indeed, it is a subject that could not in the least interest the general public. There is an old saw which runs, "Try to please and you will please." If the opposite holds good, namely, "Try not to displease and you will not displease," I shall account myself happy.

It may be asked "What is the main interest of this book?" The reader who looks for desperate adventures will be grievously disappointed. Pater slew neither lion nor centaur nor ferocious sow. No, the charm of this book—if charm it have—will be that it brings the reader into the closest possible relationship with one of the most distinguished writers of his day. Certainly it is crowded from cover to cover with good things said by Pater and his friends, and I wish the reader to feel that, with its wealth of anecdote and

c

conversation, it presents him with so much that has hitherto been unknown regarding Walter Pater—that it will seem practically an additional *Marius* or *Renaissance*—that is to say in the sense of its being a new presentment of Pater's mind.

From Pater's great friend, Mr. J. R. McQueen, I have received, as I have already mentioned, very many letters, most of which are quoted or used in my pages; but the following letter is so important that it will be better to give the portion relating to Pater *in extenso*.

"Brookhouse, Chailey, Sussex,
"17 May, 1906.

"Dear Mr. Wright,

"I *heartily* congratulate you on the great success which you have achieved in your *Life of Sir Richard Burton*, and I hope your book on Pater will be still more successful. Certainly it will contain a great deal that seems to be quite unknown to the gentlemen who have already attempted his biography. They seem to be totally ignorant of his school-life, which was really full of interest. In your biography I venture to hope you will most strongly emphasize the following particulars of Pater's boyhood:—

"1. His piety, which I am convinced was sincere, and which (with his religious feelings and studies) was a marked characteristic of Pater from the time of my first acquaintance with him till about September, 1857. It coloured and guided his whole life at that time—religion of a very High Church cast. All that period the vane of his soul was pointing S., we will say. It shifted to W. in 1857, and to N. later—taking S. to be the original religious and High Church point of the compass, and N. to be the opposite extreme of heterodoxy.

"2. Pater's liveliness and wit. He was as amusing a companion as there could be, in the days of our

PREFACE

friendship. It was almost like having a Charles Dickens' book, *viva voce,* as one's companion.

"3. His mental activity. Of course he neither did nor could write "Winckelmann," as he is fabled to have done, while he was at school, but he wrote a great deal of poetry, read a great deal, and soon after he left school was writing "Gertrude of Himmelstadt" and an "Essay on Justification." He was also, as I told you, a good actor, and in those early days it seemed to me (and to Dombrain also) that he was always imitating some favourite author—F. D. Maurice, Kingsley and others.

"I have a strong suspicion that he kept up a reserve with his Oxford friends which was wanting in his intercourse with Dombrain and myself. But I hope to say more of this in my annotations.[1] With every good wish,

"I am, yours very sincerely,
"J. R. McQueen."

The pictures in this book—some seventy in number—are of intense interest, including as they do portraits of Pater and most of his friends, and views of Weston Underwood, Harbledown, Canterbury, Oxford, and St. Austin's. Of a number of them I hold the copyright, and some are curious and scarce.

---

(1) To a copy of Mr. Benson's *Walter Pater* which Mr. McQueen sent me a few days after.

I have only, in conclusion, to give myself the pleasure of expressing my warmest thanks to all persons who have kindly assisted me in what has proved a most difficult undertaking—and especially to the following:

Adam, Rev. T. W., Hollington Rectory, Hastings.

Bathe, Rev. Anthony, Fridaythorpe Vicarage, York.
Bedson, Rev. Alfred, Osbournby Vicarage, Folkingham, S. Lincs.
Birchall, Rev. Oswald, Blackhill, Camphill, Malvern.
Biron, Rev. Henry, Lympne Vicarage, Hythe.
Bradbrook, Dr., Bletchley.
Browne, Rev. Charles H., St. Andrew's, Eastbourne.
Browning, Mr. Oscar, Cambridge.
Bussell, Rev. Dr., Brasenose College.
Bywater, Professor J., Oxford.

Campbell, Professor Lewis.
Chafy, Rev. Dr., Rous Lench Court, Evesham.
Channing, Mr. Francis Allston, M.P., 40, Eaton Place, S.W.
Collard, Sir George, Canterbury.
Comber, Mrs. (Eleanor Pater), Hughendon, Exmouth.

Fagg, Mr. John, Quarry Bank, Tonbridge.
Frend, Mr. G. H.

Galton, Rev. Arthur, Corbar Tower, Buxton.
Goodwin, Mrs. (Mira Pater), Arnold House, Lowestoft.

Hornby, Rev. Dr., Provost of Eton.

Irvine, Rev. J. W., Littlemore Vicarage, Oxford.

Jackson, Mr. Richard C.

Kearney, Rev. J. B., Cambridge.
Kearney, Miss, 146, Hills Road, Cambridge.

McQueen, Mr. John Rainier, of Braxfield, Brookhouse, Chailey, Sussex.
Magrath, Rev. Dr., Provost of Queen's College, Oxford.
Marshall, Rev. J. M., Croft Rectory, Darlington.
Matthews, Rev. W. Stabb, Briercliffe Vicarage, Burnley.
Mitchinson, The Right Rev. Bishop, Master of Pembroke College.
Monck, Rev. G. G., Closworth Rectory, Sherborne, Dorset.
Moore, Rev. Canon Edward, Principal of St. Edmund Hall, Oxford.
Moorhouse, Rev. M. B., Audley Park Gardens, Bath.
Moneypenny, Rev. P. A., Hadlow.

Nunn, Rev. J. E., Shefford, Lambourne.

Pater, Mr. Edgar Aloysius.
Pater, Mr. John E., Olney.
Later, Mr. John James, 109, Clarendon Road, Southsea.
Pater, Miss E. M., Olney.
Payne, Mr. John.

Raper, Mr. R. W., Trinity College, Oxford.
Reichel, Rev. Oswald, A la Ronde, Lympstone, Devon.
Robertson, Mr. Magnus Rainier, Chailey, Sussex.

Sayce, Rev. Professor, Queen's College, Oxford.
Sampson, Mr. C. H., Brasenose College, Oxford.
Shand, Rev. Canon, Clayton Rectory, Hassocks, Sussex.
Spain, Mr. George, 10, Victoria Square, Newcastle-on-Tyne.
Swinburne, Mr. A. C., The Pines, Putney.

PREFACE

Terrell, Mr. Gilbert A'Becket, Great Fish Hall, Hadlow.
Walker, Mr. Frank, Brasenose College.
Ward, Mr. H. Snowden, Golden Green, Hadlow.
Watson, Mr. R. Talbot.
Watts-Dunton, Mr. Theodore, The Pines, Putney.
Williams, Rev. W. S. G., Great Rollright Rectory, Chipping Norton.

The following is a fairly complete list of the Books and Magazine Articles that have been laid under contribution.

Academy, The, 15th Dec., 1870.
Alford, Life of Dean. Rivingtons.
Arnold, Matthew, by G. W. Russell.
Atlantic Monthly, Dec., 1894, Article by William Sharp.
Blackwood's Magazine, Jan., 1890.
Brasenose College, by John Buchan.
Bussell, Dr. F. W., Sermon on Pater
Canterbury Journal, File of the
Capes, Rev. W., His Various Works.
Contemporary Review, Dec., 1894.
Critical Kit-Kats, by Mr. Edmund Gosse.
Chambers's Cyclopædia of English Literature, 1906 edition. Article by Theodore Watts-Dunton, The Renascence of Wonder in Poetry.
Daily Chronicle, 7th Aug., 1904.
Fortnightly Review, Sept., 1894, Article by Lionel Johnson. Jan.—June, 1896, Article by R. J. Jacobus.
Gentleman's Magazine, Jan.—June, 1897.
Heberden, C. B., Address given at Brasenose, 27th Nov., 1904.
Jackson, Richard C., Works.
John Bull, 8th Sept., 1906.
Johnson, Lionel, "The Art of Thomas Hardy" and Poems.
Macmillan's Magazine, vol. 85, p. 193.
Mallock, Mr. W. H., *The New Republic*.
Mason, Stuart, *Oscar Wilde, &c.*
New Liberal Review, July, 1902, Article by Professor Dowden.
Nineteenth Century, Vol. 25, Jan., 1889, The Decay of Lying. Vol. 28, July—Sept., 1890, On Criticism.
Oxford Chronicle, The File of the
Pall Mall Magazine, Aug., 1904, "Avowals," by George Moore.
Pater, Walter, Works (Macmillan).
Quarterly Review, Jan., 1905.
Saturday Review, July, 1873, p. 124.
Shadwell, Dr., Translation of Dante's *Purgatorio*.
Stanley, Dean, Life and Letters.
Stories in Verse, by Rev. M. B. Moorhouse.
Symonds, John Addington, by Horatio F. Brown.
Theodore Watts-Dunton, by James Douglas.
Wilde, Oscar, Works and Magazine Articles, Life by R. H. Sherard.
Without Prejudice, by Israel Zangwill.

THOMAS WRIGHT.

CONTENTS OF VOLUME I

DEDICATION

PREFACE

CHAPTER I

THE OLD HOME AT WESTON UNDERWOOD

1.	The Buckinghamshire Paters	1
2.	The Old Home at Weston Underwood	6

CHAPTER II

4th August 1839—1844

LONDON

3.	Commercial Road, Stepney	12
4.	Death of Pater's Father, 1844; and of his Uncle, 19th September 1845	15

CHAPTER III

1844—1852

ENFIELD

5.	Chase Side	19
6.	Aunt Bessie, Cats	22
7.	Death of the Grandmother, 21st February 1848	24
8.	Fish Hall	25
9.	Hadlow	29

CHAPTER IV

1853

FIRST YEAR AT THE KING'S SCHOOL

10.	Harbledown	33
11.	Canterbury	34
12.	Rev. George Wallace	39
13.	The King's School	40
14.	The Assistant Masters	44

CHAPTER V
1853
SCHOOL ANECDOTES

15.	The Snow Fights	51
16.	Snakes	52
17.	Tip and Nep	55
18.	Mrs. Norton's Stall; Mr. Teal	56
19	Boating	59
20.	A. P. Stanley	60

CHAPTER VI
1853
IN THE CATHEDRAL

21.	A Saint's Day. Punch	64
22.	The Bell Harry Tower	70

CHAPTER VII
1854
DEATH OF PATER'S MOTHER

23.	Death of Pater's Mother, 5th February 1854	74
24.	Hursley and Keble	77
25.	Henry Dombrain, February 1854	78
26.	The Speech Day, 28th September 1854	79

CHAPTER VIII
1855
J. R. MCQUEEN

27.	John Rainier McQueen, 6th February 1855	84
28.	The Triumvirate	87
29.	Pater "the Saintly Boy"	89

CHAPTER IX
1855
THE REV. GEORGE WALLACE AGAIN

30.	The Rev. George Wallace	92
31.	Pater's Rival	93
32.	Emerald Uthwart	94
33.	The Warrior's Chapel	95
34.	Joseph Haydock	96
35.	The School Speech Day, September 1855	97

CONTENTS

CHAPTER X
January—May 1856
S. ELIZABETH

36. S. Elizabeth (January 1856) and other poems. Mira - 98

CHAPTER XI
May 1856
THE BLEAN WOODS

37. The Blean Woods; Blaxlands - - - - 104
38. The Hospital of St. Nicholas - - - - - 106
39. Bishopsbourne - - - - - - 107
40. The Peace Rejoicings, 29th May 1856 - - - 108
41. High Church - - - - - - - 109

CHAPTER XII
July—December 1856
A SERIOUS ILLNESS

42. Pater injured in a Scuffle, August 1856 - - - 110
43. The School Speech Day, September 1856. Mr. Sankey leaves 111

CHAPTER XIII
January and February 1857
DEATH OF DEAN LYALL

44. Death of Dean Lyall, February 1857 - - - - 112
45. Dean Alford, 6th March 1857 - - - - - 113
46. Rev. John Bachelor Kearney; Mrs. Rainier - - - 117

CHAPTER XIV
March 1857—July 1857
CASSANDRA

47. Cassandra, 29th June 1857 - - - - - 118
48. School Speech Day, 6th August 1857 - - - 119
49. Pater and Dickens - - - - - - 123

CHAPTER XV
August 1857
CHAILEY

50. Brookhouse, August 1857 - - - - - 125

xxvi. LIFE OF WALTER PATER

CHAPTER XVI.
August to December 1857
MISS GABRIEL

51.	Miss Virginia Gabriel, August 1857	132
52.	Admitted to the Year of Grace, December 1857	132
53.	Departure of Canon Stanley, March 1858	133

CHAPTER XVII
January—October 1858
SWEET SIRMIO, ADIEU

54.	Watchman! what of the night? Summer 1858	136
55.	The Speech Day, 5th August 1858	139
56.	The Blaxlands Incident, 6th August 1858	143

CHAPTER XVIII
14 October 1858—November 1858
QUEEN'S COLLEGE, OXFORD

57.	Tears at Oxford, 14th October 1858	145
58.	The Oxford of 1858	146
59.	The Eyrie at Queen's	153
60.	The Rev. W. W. Capes	154
61.	Canon Stanley again	156
62.	Pater the Thrifty	160

CHAPTER XIX
December 1858—February 1859
HEIDELBERG

63.	M. B. Moorhouse and "Sconcing"	161
64.	Christmas at Heidelberg: S. Gertrude of Himmelstadt	162
65.	Fair Cousins. "Brimstone and Treacle"	164

CHAPTER XX
February and March 1859
BREAKING WITH CHRISTIANITY

66.	F. D. Maurice, Breaking with Christianity, February 1859	167
67.	Maol-ciaran, The Reconciliation, March 1859	170
68.	Pater and McQueen at Cumnor, 5th March 1859	171

CHAPTER XXI
April 1859—August 1859
OXFORD FRIENDS

69.	Browning and Matthew Arnold	172
70.	J. W. Hoole and Byronic Wood, April 1859 A Four to Godstowe	174

CONTENTS

71.	Commemoration Day, 1859	175
72.	The Romance of the King's School, 11th June 1859	177
73.	At Heidelburg again, Worms and Spires, July—September 1859	178

CHAPTER XXII

15th August 1859—December 1859

THE REV. E. H. WOODALL

74.	The Rev. E. H. Woodall goes over to Rome, 15th August 1859	180
75.	The Acorn, October 1859	181
76.	The Fan of Fire, November 1859	182
77.	At Mainz and Antwerp, 1st November 1859	183
78.	Back at Oxford	184
79.	Christmas with Dombrain and the Threat of Rev. J. B. Kearney and McQueen, December 1859	188
80.	The Books he read	190

CHAPTER XXIII

January 1860—October 1860

THE MOUSTACHE

81.	A Story of a Moustache	192
82.	"Oxford Life," March 1860	193
83.	The Influence of Jowett	195

CHAPTER XXIV

October 1860—October 1862

84.	Pater burns his Manuscripts	199
85.	The Triumvirate is dissolved, Autumn 1860	200
86.	The Rev. Thomas Chamberlain	201
87.	Pater and M. B. Moorhouse	202
88.	Darwin	203
89.	W. K. W. Chafy and Dombrain	204

CHAPTER XXV

MCQUEEN AND THE BISHOP OF LONDON

October 1862—5th February 1864

90.	The Final Exam.	206
91.	McQueen's Letter, December 1862 The Old Morta'ity Society	207
92.	Death of Aunt Bessie	209

CHAPTER XXVI

5th February 1864 to February 1866

THE CRYSTAL MAN

93.	Probationary Fellow of Brasenose, 5th February 1864	211
94.	Brasenose College	212
95.	Pater's Rooms	215
96.	The Crystal Man, 1864	216
97.	Actual Fellow, 5th February 1865	221
98.	In Italy with C. L. Shadwell, 1865	225
99.	The Influence of Coleridge, January 1866	225

CHAPTER XXVII

February 1866—13th November 1870

ART FOR ART'S SAKE

100.	Art for Art's Sake	229
101.	The Swinburnian Fever	230
102.	Winckelmann, January 1867 Oscar Browning	232
103.	Pater no Scholar. No. 2 Bradmore Road	236
104.	Richard Robinson, 13th November 1870	240

CHAPTER XXVIII

13th November 1870—December 1873

THE RENAISSANCE

105.	Humanism	243
106.	Burn with a Gem-like Flame	245
107.	Mr. and Mrs. Mark Pattison	252

CHAPTER XXIX

JOWETT'S SALUTARY WHIP

1874

108.	Jowett's Salutary Whip	255
109.	Mr. Edmund Gosse, Mandell Creighton, Rev. Lewis Campbell	259
110.	T. H. Green, Mr. and Mrs. Humphry Ward	260

LIST OF PLATES IN VOLUME I.

		PAGE
1.	Walter Pater: *From Oxford Characters*	*Frontispiece*
2.	"The Knobs"	3
3.	The Pater Tombstones	3
4.	The Old Home of the Paters	7
5.	Token Issued by a Buckingham Lace-Buyer	13
6.	A Buckinghamshire Lace-Maker and Girl Winding Thread	13
7.	Mr. William Pater	17
8.	Fish Hall, Hadlow, Kent	27
9.	A King's School Boy	32
10.	Rev. George Wallace, M.A.	37
11.	Dr. Reinhold Rost	41
12.	Rev. Anby Beatson	41
13.	The Home of the Pater Family	45
14.	The King's School, Canterbury.—The School House	50
15.	The King's School, Canterbury.—The Mint Yard	53
16.	The King's School, Canterbury.—Norman Staircase to the Schoolroom	57
17.	The King's School, Canterbury.—From the Green Court	61
18.	The Green Court, Canterbury	67
19.	The Procession to the Cathedral	71
20.	Grave of Pater's Mother	75
21.	A Speech Day in the Chapter House, Canterbury	81
22.	Rev. John Bachelor Kearney	115
23.	M. Martinet	115
24.	View in the Grounds of Brookhouse, Chailey, Sussex	122
25.	Brookhouse, Chailey	122
26.	Chailey Church	127
27.	Queen's College, Oxford	147
28.	Queen's College, Oxford.—Back Quadrangle	151
29.	Queen's College, Oxford.—The Chapel	157
30.	J. Rainier McQueen	185
31.	Henry Dombrain	185
32.	Rev. Canon Shand	213
33.	Rev. Dr. Hornby in 1866	213
34.	Brasenose College, Oxford, showing Pater's Rooms	219
35.	Brasenose College from Radcliffe Square	223
36.	Pater's Sitting-Room at Brasenose	227
37.	2, Bradmore Road, Norham Gardens, Oxford	233
38.	Rev. A. J. Dodgson (Lewis Carroll)	237
39.	Mr. Richard Robinson	237
40.	Walter Pater.—*From an Oil Painting by Mr. W. S. Wright*	247
41.	Walter Pater.—*From a Group Taken at Brasenose*	247
42.	Mr. Edmund Gosse	257

THE LIFE OF WALTER PATER.

CHAPTER I

THE OLD HOME AT WESTON UNDERWOOD

The Paters are of Dutch descent, though the family must have settled in England at a very early date—perhaps in the reign of Elizabeth, for there were Paters resident in Thornton,[1] Buckinghamshire, within a year or two of her death; though whether or not Walter Pater was descended from this stock, it is impossible to say. The fact, however, that Pater was of Dutch lineage should be constantly borne in mind by those who wish to understand his temperament and character.

1. The Buckinghamshire Paters.

In everything done by the Dutch there is, to use Pater's words, a "minute and scrupulous air of caretaking and neatness;"[2] and of the work of Pater himself the same might be truthfully said. He was correct even to painfulness. But he had, as his friend Mr. McQueen reminds the writer, "another attribute of the Dutch and Frisian races—extreme obstinacy and wilfulness." Indeed he was almost as much a Dutchman as if he had been born, like his Sebastian van Storck, among the eerie Hobbema trees and the rich-coloured

---

[1] For particulars of the Thornton Paters see our Appendix.
[2] *Imag. Portraits*, p. 10.

Van de Velde shipping of Haarlem and the Zuider Zee. In the bustling seventeenth century there was an Admiral Pater, of whom, however, we have no information except that his grateful country rewarded him, for doing nothing in particular, with a handsome salary. Then one recalls Jean Baptiste Pater,[1] the artist, many of whose delicate, sparkling, summer-day paintings may be seen in the Wallace Gallery; and possibly both these rather nebulous personages sprang from the same old Dutch stock that produced Walter Pater. The pleasure that Pater found in the belief that he was connected with Jean Baptiste Pater is reflected in that dainty prose-poem, "A Prince of Court Painters," [2] which hymns the romantic friendship between Watteau and his less though, nevertheless, remarkably gifted, pupil.

The Paters from whom Walter Pater was undoubtedly descended are first heard of in our own little Holland—the Norfolk and Suffolk sea-board—where there was a complete Dutch colony, as the solid but picturesque old houses still to be seen on Yarmouth Quay bear sufficient witness.

One branch, settled at Beccles, was engaged in the lace trade—then regarded as purely a gentleman's occupation—their business being to collect the lace from the village makers and take it periodically to the London markets; and like many other lace-merchants they accumulated wealth. In the eighteenth century a Thompson Pater (Thompson Pater the First) married a Miss Mary Church, whose mother was a member of the old Norfolk and Catholic family of Gage; and by-and-by we find this Thompson Pater settled first at Newport Pagnell,[3] and afterwards at Weston

---

[1] Jean Baptiste Joseph Pater, 1695—1736, friend of Watteau. Painted "Conversation Galante," &c. See Walter Pater's *Imaginary Portraits*.

[2] In *Imaginary Portraits*.

[3] Mary Pater is described on her tombstone in Weston Underwood churchyard as being the widow of Thompson Pater, "formerly of Newport Pagnell."

THE PATER TOMBSTONES.
WESTON UNDERWOOD CHURCHYARD.
Photo by Mr. E. Beesly.

"THE KNOBS."
ENTRANCE TO WESTON UNDERWOOD.
Photo by Mr. Philip A. Wright.

Underwood near Olney—the family having been drawn thither owing to the great advantage the district offered in that it was the centre of the lace trade. At Newport Pagnell, Thompson Pater was nine miles from the Thornton Paters, who, as we said, may or may not have been closely related to him. From that time downwards there have always been Paters at Weston Underwood and Olney, where the family is at the present day abundantly represented. Olney and Weston Underwood, it is almost superfluous to observe, are chiefly famous by reason of their connection with the poet Cowper, who resided at Olney from 1767 to 1786, and at Weston from 1786 to 1795; consequently the Paters, to use Walter Pater's expression, "nested" long in the midst of that country which is delineated in the delicate vignettes of *The Task* and in the charming letters of the half-playful, half-pathetic correspondent of Lady Hesketh and William Hayley.

At the north-east end of the village stood Weston Hall, the seat of Cowper's friends, the courtly Catholic Throckmortons, who were lords of the manor;[1] and the chapel attended by them and the Paters was a wing of the old mansion.[2] At the south-west of the village is the Protestant Church of St. Lawrence, under the shadow of whose cupola-capped tower may be seen a line of grey lichen-stained stones to various members of the Pater family, each beseeching, in dimly legible words, the pious loiterer to "Pray for the souls" of those commemorated.

[1] Sir Robert Throckmorton, 4th baronet, died 1791; Sir John Courtenay Throckmorton, 5th baronet, died 1819; Sir George Courtenay Throckmorton, 6th baronet, died 1826. The two latter were Cowper's friends.

[2] Nothing now remains of Weston Hall except the granary, surmounted by a cupola, and the gateways with stone piers. The grounds, however, laid out by Lancelot Brown, are glorious as ever. About half the inhabitants of the village were Roman Catholics.

The home of the Paters was the fine Tudor house with tiled roof, heavily mullioned windows and great gateway with massive piers surmounted by stone balls, standing in the narrow lane which joins the village street close to the socket of the ancient wayside cross. This lane was formerly part of the main road from Olney, which in those days passed at the back of Weston Hall —that is to say between the Hall and the River Ouse. Walter Pater amused himself with the notion that Miss Mary Church was the first to introduce Roman Catholicism into the family, but the Weston and Olney Paters stoutly affirm—and there is no gainsaying their evidence—that he was in error, and that the Paters were always of the more ancient faith. As regards the family of Thompson Pater the First, the sons were brought up Protestants, the daughters Catholics. Thompson Pater's children were Elizabeth Enser Gage [1] [1765— ?], John Thompson [1766—1812], Mary [2] [1768— ?], Ann [3] [1769—1850], John James [1772— ?], John Church [4] [1775— ?], Martha [5] [1776—1847], and Lydia. On one of the tombstones at Weston Underwood a Mrs. Timson, daughter of Thompson and Mary Pater, is mentioned, but her christian name is unknown unless she and Lydia are the same.

2. **The Old Home at Weston Underwood.**

The poet Cowper, on being lured, in 1786, by Lady Hesketh and the Throckmortons from "Orchard Side," Olney, to the loftier Weston Underwood, took up his residence at Weston Lodge, a spacious house situated

---

[1] Baptised at Weston 14th March 1765, confirmed at Weston 4th October 1778. A small silver spoon, with her name and the date 1773, used to be in the possession of Walter Pater.

[2] Baptised at Weston 5th March 1768.

[3] Confirmed at Weston 4th October 1778. Buried at Weston.

[4] A christening mug, with his name and the date 1775, is in the possession of Miss Emma Pater of Olney.

[5] Baptised at Weston 14th October 1776, by Wm. Gregson. Buried at Weston.

THE OLD HOME OF THE PATERS
AT WESTON UNDERWOOD, NEAR OLNEY, BUCKS.

Photo by Mr. Lett, Olney.

in the middle of the village; and Thompson Pater and his daughters Martha and Ann, were, a few years later, on terms of intimacy with both him and Mrs. Unwin; while Ann Pater, an enthusiastic admirer of the poet, treasured some original verses which he had given her. Other intimate friends of the Paters were Doctor William Gregson [1] the priest (Cowper's "Greggy") *"pauperum medicus et amicus,"* as he is affectionately called on his memorial tablet at Weston, and the Rev. John Buchanan,[2] the Protestant curate (Cowper's "Buchy").

As years advanced the family became scattered. Only Martha and Ann remained at Weston—Ann, "the intellectual sister," being remembered by venerable inhabitants of Olney as "a buxom and very stately dame who wore 'a brooch' (fastening a silk ribbon) on the middle of her forehead"; a cap with Weston-made lace frilling round her face, and under her chin," and a silk dress which always looked new and "crackled" as she walked. To privileged persons (and one was an Olney jeweller who is still living) the important old lady condescended to show her principal heirloom—a casket of precious stones; and we also hear of another treasure which for several generations was carefully handed down from father to son—a china bowl representing a Race Meeting.[3]

We said that the Paters were lace buyers and that like so many other lace buyers they accumulated wealth. We please ourselves with the assumption that they were fair, and even generous, to the poor pinched workers, whose fate, indeed—as the distressing pictures in

---

[1] Dr. William Gregson was priest at Weston from 1770 to 1800. He died 18th October 1800, aged 68. He was gifted as a physician as well as a priest, hence the phrase on his tablet.

[2] Rev. John Buchanan died 3rd December 1826, aged 74.

[3] Now in the possession of Mr. John James Pater of Southsea, to whom it was given by Mr. John Pater of Trinity College, Oxford.

Cowper's letters, the somewhat brighter sketch in his poem entitled *Truth,* and the pitiful tales of old inhabitants sufficiently testify—was indeed a saddening one. The picturesqueness of the occupation however —and men and boys as well as women and girls used, as Cowper said, "to dandle the pillow"—has diverted attention from its dark and sordid accompaniments. We are apt to think only of the comely woman (seated in a honeysuckle bower and under a caged magpie), with her pillow, pillow-horse, gaily spangled bobbins, serried regiments of pins, and delicate, cobwebby Buckinghamshire "point"—shown to the curious over dark blue paper; or of the same worker on some "unked" (always their word) winter's evening planted with others round the flasked candle-stool,* with brown pipkins (filled with hot wood ashes) at their feet, while the monotone of the "Lace Tells"[1] mingles with the creak of the bobbin-winder. Cowper, himself, indeed, as may be judged from one of his rarest passages, was better pleased to dwell on the simple pleasures of the lace-makers than on their woes. He says—

> Yon cottager, who weaves at her own door,
> Pillow and bobbins all her little store;
> Content, though mean; and cheerful, if not gay:
> Shuffling her threads about the live-long day,
> Just earns a scanty pittance, and at night
> Lies down secure, her heart and pocket light.

But thanks to the ministrations of John Newton, Thomas Scott, and other noble men who for years occupied the pulpits and visited the cottages of Olney and Weston, the poor toiler knows her Bible thoroughly—

> And in that charter reads with sparkling eyes,
> Her title to a treasure in the skies.

* The flasks reflected the light on to the work.

[1] Songs sung over the pillow. In the lace schools the proficiency of the worker was estimated by the number of pins stuck in in a given time. The singing of these Tells assisted the counting. But most workers used to sing at their work.

It is probable, even, that much of the lace sold by the Paters was made in Cowper's own house at Olney [1] for that building was, after Cowper's departure, converted into a lace school, and the thin shrill voices of mites of five and six could any day, and almost at any time between twilight and twilight,[2] be heard singing, as their baby fingers deftly shifted the bobbins—

> "Dingle dangle, farthing candle,"
>
> "Nineteen miles to Spangle Church,"
>
> "Up the street and down the street,
>   With windows made of glass,"

or one of the many other ill-rhyming but favourite "Tells"[3]—the singing being always followed by a dead silence, during which a certain number of pins—called a "glum"—were stuck in; when the thin voices would once more pipe out with the same or some new ditty.

Another pleasant link between Cowper and the Paters was their common love for the Dutchman's pride and darling—the tulip. Though the mania for high-priced bulbs had by that time considerably cooled, the best families of the Olney neighbourhood still plumed themselves on their tulip beds, and Cowper's remark after a visit to the great splashes of scarlet, amber, and bistre at Emberton Rectory has often been quoted—"A fine painting, and God the artist!"

[1] Cowper's House at Olney was in 1900 presented to the Town and Nation by the late Mr. W. H. Collingridge, and it is now *The Cowper Museum*, with a very rich collection of Cowper manuscripts, pictures, and other valuable objects of Cowperian interest.

[2] In the summer the hours were very long. Work began at five—sometimes even at four—in the morning.

[3] The elder girls usually favoured the "Love Tells," that is to say, the verses in which they could insert the name of their sweetheart.

CHAPTER II

4TH AUGUST 1839 TO 1844

LONDON

Thompson Pater the Second, the brother of Ann and Martha Pater, married a Miss Hester Grange, and went out to New York, whence, with his three children—Elizabeth, Richard Glode and William, he, after a while, found his way back to London, where he practised as a surgeon until his death in 1812, at the early age of 46.[1] His two sons followed their father's profession, and ultimately settled in partnership as surgeons in Marine Place, Commercial Road, Stepney—their sister residing with them. Richard, who had already quitted the Catholic Church, married a Miss Maria Hill, and had four children—William Thompson 1835 (as we have seen, there had for long been a Thompson in the family), Walter Horatio, subject of this work, and two daughters. Walter, born 4 August, 1839, and named after his cousin and godmother, Mrs. Walter Horatio May, of Fish Hall, Tonbridge, had a slightly misformed back, and was of a curiously unprepossessing appearance, being a remarkable contrast to his brother William, whose early beauty was remarkable, and who grew to be an extremely handsome man. The misformed back was a feature rather common in the family. Pater's aunt Bessie, for example, had it; and the Paters, who were rather proud of it than not, called it prettily "the Pater Poke."

3. Commercial Road, Stepney.

---

[1] His widow, who outlived him 36 years, died 21st February 1848, aged 81, and was buried at Enfield. See Chapter III.

TOKEN ISSUED BY A BUCKINGHAM LACE-BUYER.

A BUCKINGHAMSHIRE LACE-MAKER AND GIRL
WINDING THREAD.

Photo by Mr. W. S. Wright.

It is almost superfluous to point out that other men of genius besides Pater have been plain—Goldsmith and Gibbon for example; and Mr. Augustine Birrell goes so far as to declare that "male ugliness is an endearing quality, and in a man of great talents it assists his reputation. It mollifies our inferiority to be able to add to our honest admiration of anyone's great intellectual merit, 'But did you ever see such a chin!' ";[1] and has not Emerson observed, "If a man can raise a small city to be a great kingdom . . can lead the opinions of mankind . . 'tis no matter whether his nose is parallel to his spine as it ought to be or whether he has a nose at all . . all deformities will come to be reckoned ornamental and advantageous on the whole?" [2]

The London Paters were of the order of mortals who, in Lord Byron's phrase, become "old in their youth and die in middle age."[3] As we have noticed, Thompson, Walter Pater's grandfather, died at 46, and both Walter Pater's father and his uncle passed away at the same age. Pater's brother, as we shall see, reached only 52, Pater himself only 55. On the decease of Pater's father—"a tall grave figure, a little cold and severe"[4]—in 1844, Mrs. Pater and her children, Mr. Pater's sister Elizabeth (Aunt Bessie) and Mrs. Thompson Pater (Walter's grandmother) removed to a small house in Chase Side, Enfield—the Chase Lodge of "Emerald Uthwart;" [5] where they lived upon a very modest income. To both his grandmother and his Aunt Bessie—"a very lady-like little crouched figure, who won the love of all who knew her"—Walter became deeply attached; and he just remembered his

4. Death of Pater's Father 1844, and of his Uncle 19th Sept. 1845.

[1] *Res Judicatæ*, p. 66.
[2] *Conduct of Life*: Beauty.
[3] *Manfred*.
[4] See *Marius*, Vol. I., p. 10.
[5] *Miscellaneous Studies*, p. 170.

Uncle William, a gentle, cultured man—much given, like the rest of his race, to the study of Cowper—who used to express the hope that he would pass his last days under the beeches and alders of Weston Underwood, and be buried among his kin by the cupola-capped tower. But the Fates decreed otherwise, for he died suddenly at Marine Place, 19th September, 1845,[1] leaving an only daughter Mira,[2] aged three; and he was laid by the side of his brother in a London churchyard.[3] Walter, as he grew older found pleasure, like his Duke Carl,[4] in enquiring about his ancestors and connections—information relative to whom, their wealth, and their ways filtered to him chiefly through his Aunt Bessie; and here and there in his works we are reminded of the Weston associations—as for example in the title of his autobiographical sketch "Emerald Uthwart," a name suggested, doubtless, by the ancient and honourable Uthwatt family settled at Great Linford, Bucks., friends of the Paters. Still, neither Weston, nor the winding Ouse, nor the poet Cowper ever attracted him; and in after life the last became one of his special antipathies.

[1] "In Marine-pl., Commercial-road, aged 45, Dr. W. G. Pater." *Gentleman's Magazine, November* 1845.

[2] Now Mrs. Goodwin.

[3] His widow became Mrs. Bloomfield. During her second widowhood she lived much with Mrs. May, *née* Porter, of Fish Hall.

[4] *Imaginary Portraits*, p. 136. This book contains much of Pater's own history.

MR. WILLIAM PATER.

FROM A MINIATURE LENT BY MRS. GOODWIN (MIRA PATER).

CHAPTER III

1844 TO 1852

ENFIELD

Enfield,[1] "a little place in the neighbourhood of a great city," was in Walter Pater's childhood an old-fashioned village, with quaint Annian houses, an ancient church surrounded by "dark cavernous shops," a market cross, a venerable King James and Tinker Inn, and the hoary relics of the mansion of King John shadowed by immemorial cedars. It was already a classic spot. Here John Keats spent his school-days (1802 to 1810); and from 1827 to 1833 it was the home of Charles Lamb, one of Pater's warmest enthusiasms.[2]

5. Chase Side.

The house in which the Paters lived was situated, as we said, in Chase Side—a street nearly a mile long, which, however, contained then only a few houses, most of them ancient. If the reader, fresh from "Emerald Uthwart" and "The Child in the House" imagines the Pater's home as the manorial seat of a country gentleman he is peculiarly in error. It was, indeed, but a small, decorous, white tenement, both house and garden being as narrow as the means of their occupants. The houses[3] in "Emerald Uthwart" and "The Child in the House" are less the Paters' house at Enfield than what, in Pater's opinion, that

---

[1] Pater pays a tribute to its attractions at the end of his article on "Charles Lamb." *Appreciations*, p. 122.

[2] *Appreciations*, p. 105. Lamb died at Edmonton in 1835. His house is still standing.

[3] These, as we shall show, were compounds of the house in Chase Side, Fish Hall, and Brookhouse, Chailey.

house ought to have been. And this is the key to all the quasi-autobiographical elements in his works. He gives not so much himself and his surroundings as his ideals. His own lineage and home not being to his taste, he very sensibly has himself, in the character of Emerald and Florian, born over again, and in better circumstances—that is to say in a goodly Manor House, with the suggestion of ancestors who in mail and morion lie handsomely on their backs on sculptured altar tombs. Yet Emerald and Florian are certainly Walter Pater, or rather Walter Pater with a straight back and even features.[1] Every person whose imaginary portrait Pater drew is a gentleman both by birth and pocket—Marius, Sebastian, Florian, Duke Carl, Emerald—all of them; and to each is allotted, in addition to certain of Pater's qualities, the various qualities, and possessions, and the atmosphere that Pater coveted. Pater, indeed, who thought meanly of the tradesman, and could barely tolerate the merchant, valued none but the courtly gentleman with a comfortable rent roll; and held, very properly, with Cowper, that "poverty is the most indelicate thing in the world." [2]

If, however, the house in Chase Side was mean, it was pleasantly situated, and the long ribbon of garden in front was odorous with wallflowers and sweet peas. Pater, now a little weazened man rather than a child (for he had been born as it were with down on his chin, and, like the rest of his race, had ripened prematurely), dearly loved both house and garden. The house, he assures us, acted to his wandering soul "as, in the second degree, its body and earthly tabernacle." Thus

---

[1] We must here enter a protest against the insipid, spiritless portraits of Pater, or rather the portraits of somebody called Pater, with all the irregularities of his face smoothed out. We object to seeing Cromwell without his warts, Sir Richard Burton without his "devil's jaw." We also object to see Pater pourtrayed as the good-looking but expressionless young man who hands things about with so much grace at a garden party.

[2] To Mrs. Throckmorton, 19th February 1791.

"The Child in the House"; and in the Essay on Rossetti the thought is repeated—"the house . . . grown now to be a kind of raiment to one's body, as the body, according to Swedenborg, is but the raiment of the soul." Then, too, how lovingly he speaks of the wallflower that scented the garden—"*Flos Parietis,* as he and his brother had been taught to call it."[1] Close by stood, in its own grounds, a large and venerable mansion inhabited by a gentleman who had adopted a nephew named, at first, Howgrave, and afterwards Graham. Graham became Pater's playmate, and taught him, among other accomplishments, how to make flowers of sealing-wax. They both found the pastime amusing, until Pater dropped some hot wax on his hand, and then it was amusing only to Graham. Finally Pater burnt his hand badly, with the result of the "languid scent of ointments put upon the place to make it well,"[2] and a sleepless night.

Pater's favourite amusement, however, was playing at being a clergyman,[3] and getting Graham and other lads to form a procession. There was a tiny, darkish, and almost useless room at the back of the house, and here, arrayed in a nightgown for surplice, he preached regularly and with unction to his mother, grandmother, and his admiring Aunt Bessie. To this amusement, as it required neither sealing-wax nor "languid scent of ointments," they never offered objection. His aunt, indeed, was as pleased to listen as he to preach, and he could usually—wet or fine—depend on a congregation of one. In idea, she saw him a real clergyman, and she never ceased to pray that he might take Holy Orders. Sometimes she even imagined him an archbishop, for

---

[1] "Child in the House, *Miscellaneous Studies*, p. 150. See, too, "Emerald Uthwart," *Miscellaneous Studies*, p. 175.

[2] See "Emerald Uthwart."

[3] There are several allusions to this in Pater's works *c.f. Marius,* vol. I., p. 132. "Those childish days of reverie when he played at priests." Pater told Mr. McQueen that this was his favourite game at Enfield.

he was just ten years old, and both the archbishops of that day, it seems, had once been ten, and both were distinctly out of the upright. The patience of the dear soul, however, was often sadly tried, for Pater, who had a mania for the game, wanted to play every day. Like the infantile Chevalier in a favourite book of his later years, *Manon Lescaut,* he "thought of nothing but becoming a clergyman," and for such un-clerical pursuits as top-spinning and marbles, which were indulged in by Graham and other worldly-minded boys, he had nothing but good-natured contempt. He remembered with pleasure, however, Graham's garden, as he remembered his own. "How they shook their musk from them!—those gardens!"[1]

His aunt Bessie—patient and painstaking woman—taught him to read, while his canary in its cage hopped from perch to perch, and the perfume of the lime tree in the garden fell through the air upon them like rain; and when he grew older he received instruction from the head master of Enfield Grammar School. Besides his canary he had a starling, which, however, out of pity, he set free. But the chief object of his affection was a beautiful white Angora, "with a dark tail like an ermine's, and a face like a flower"—the first of a long series of cats. The cat, indeed, life through, was to Pater what the owl was to Minerva, the hare to Cowper. He was never without one, and often he had several. How pleasantly he introduces Pussy at the Apuleian feast in *Marius.* Indeed, Pater himself was very much like a cat—a quiet, gentle, lovable, blinking, purring, velvet-footed creature—only his face was not "like a flower."

6. Aunt Bessie. Cats.

As the boy grew older two predominant processes of mental change—to use his own expression—could be noted in him.[2] "The growth of an almost diseased

---

[1] *Miscellaneous Studies,* p. 172.
[2] "Child in the House," *Miscellaneous Studies,* p. 155.

sensibility to the spectacle of suffering, and parallel with this, the rapid growth of a certain capacity of fascination by bright colour and choice form . . . marking early the activity in him of a more than customary sensuousness, 'the lust of the eye.'" The fear of death came upon him early, and his thoughts wandered often upon ghosts—the returning dead—whom he would fancy on wild nights "pathetically as crying, or beating with vain hands at the doors." [1] He delighted especially in St. Andrew's Church—the old parish church of Enfield, and he used to climb its giddy winding stair up to the pigeons and the bells. He loved processions, "holy days, all that belonged to the comely order of the sanctuary." In *The Child in the House* [2] he pictured himself at his mother's side on a summer's day in this churchyard. "In a bright dress he rambled among the graves, in the gay weather, and so came, in one corner, upon an open grave for a child—a dark space on the brilliant grass . . . . And therewith came, full-grown, never wholly to leave him, with the certainty that even children do sometimes die, the physical horror of death."

Bible messengers became very real to him, and he would have met without surprise by the New River or at Enfield Market Cross, angels such as talked to Abraham, and wrestled with Jacob. If under an oak at Hebron, why not under Dr. Robert Uvedale's great cedar at "Enfield Palace?" Nay, he sometimes alleged that he had seen them.

Then, too, he had a passion for everything white. We have noticed his white cat, and certainly one of the charms of being a little clergyman was wearing a white surplice. In *The Child in the House*—in all his works indeed—we learn how the "comely whiteness"

[1] *Miscellaneous Studies* ("The Child in the House"), p. 155. So too in *Marius*, vol. I., p. 11, the dead genii . . . would be heard . . . crying sorrowfully in the stillness of the night.

[2] *Miscellaneous Studies*, p. 163.

of things pleases him. Even the mice that run wild in the attic are white. White mice, however, do not run about a house unless some one introduces them; and Walter probably knew better than any one else how they came there. As he grew older this passion for whiteness and cleanness increased. He stands for white marble. He is the Alma-Tadema of English Literature.

There now occurred two deaths in the family—the first being that, at Weston Underwood, of Pater's great aunt Martha;[1] but whatever expectations her relatives at Chase Side had from her were doomed to disappointment, for, unhappily, none of her money drifted thither. She is buried at Weston Underwood, her superiority to the common flesh lying about her being indicated by the word "Miss"[2] inscribed on her tombstone. The second death was that of Mrs. Thompson Pater, Walter's grandmother, who, as we have seen, had for several years lived with his mother and aunt. The event ate itself into his memory, and in *The Child in the House* he speaks of the cry on the stair[3]—the voice of his aunt Bessie—"sounding bitterly through the house" when his grandmother breathed her last; moreover, in *Gaston de Latour* he pays a well-deserved tribute to her memory. The "old grandmother died, to the undissembled sorrow of Gaston, bereft, unexpectedly as it seemed, of the gentle creature to whom he had always turned for an affection that had been as no other in its absolute incapacity of offence." Mrs. Thompson Pater was

7. Death of his Grandmother, 21st Feb., 1848.

---

[1] She died 1st February 1847, and is buried at Weston Underwood. Her sister Ann lived till 1860.

[2] In those days ladies of means or pretensions were described on their tombstones as "Miss" or "Mrs.," with the Christian name. The poor had to be content with the Christian name only.

[3] In "The Child in the House" it is Florian's father who dies. *Miscellaneous Studies*, p. 157.

buried at Enfield Parish Church, where there is a tombstone to her memory, with the following inscription—

SACRED
To the Memory of
MRS. HESTER PATER,
Relict of the late
MR. THOMPSON PATER, Surgeon,
of the Commercial Road, London,
and Mother of the late
RICHARD and WILLIAM PATER,
Surgeons, of the same place.
Died February 21st, 1848.
Aged 81.

Sometimes Walter and his brother paid a visit to Fishall Hall, for short Fish Hall,[1] Hadlow, near Tonbridge, a fine old Georgian cube of red brick, the residence of his cousin, Mr. **8. Fish Hall.** Walter Horatio May; and of this there are some reminiscences in *The Child in the House,* though Florian's home certainly bears much more resemblance to a house at Chailey,[2] presently to be described. The comely whiteness about the place would alone exclude Fish Hall, where everything is aggressively red. Red bricks, red walls, red tiles. Fish Hall is approached from the public road by a long drive, bordered with ornamental shrubs and pampas grass. Here and there the exterior has been restored, but the original work predominates, while its three or four unmistakably sham windows remind of the days of the tax. When we visited the house at the end of 1903 we had the opportunity of exploring it, as Pater must so often have done, from cellar to roof. The largest room on the ground floor is panelled from floor to ceiling with oak, and the old boxing shutters still remain. All the bedroom floors bow in the middle, and everything trembles if you set down your

[1] Now the residence of Gilbert à Becket Terrell, Esq.
[2] See Chapter XI.

foot smartly; while none of the doors, made of elm rudely planed, hang straight; and the boards of which they are formed have shrunk so much that you could put your hand between them. The ceilings of the highest storey are shored up to prevent them from falling; everywhere the woodwork is warped; and there are, in all sorts of unexpected places, all sorts of extraordinary "fripperies,"[1] or room-like cupboards, through which the bed chambers communicate with one another.

An ideal place for hide and seek! But Walter never played that undignified game, or, indeed, any other game, except that of pretending to be a clergyman; and "fripperies" are useless to the cloth except as vestries—of which the most extravagant of clergymen would not require thirty-nine. We crept up some steps into the "cockloft,"[2] and by aid of a candle picked our way among great worm-eaten beams, along a crazy floor, black with bat droppings, and through a small opening on to the roof, which is of the Mansard type, partly leaded, partly tiled. Here we noticed a fire or alarm bell, with date 1812, the clapper of which had fallen from its place on to the leads; while the corners of the house gave evidence of ball terminals.

A short distance from the house are three great ponds surrounded with alders and yews, under whose tremulous boughs moved a flotilla of stately swans. Another feature of the grounds is a treillaged walk, making a delightful perspective of greenery; and there is a decrepit mulberry tree, whose aged limbs are supported by strong timbers. Such is Fish Hall—the enchantment of Walter Pater's boyhood. He loved, in his contemplative way, to roam through its maze of rooms, passages, and

[1] Small rooms used as wardrobes.
[2] The name given to the inverted V-shaped space just under the roof.

FISH HALL, HADLOW, KENT.

FROM A PHOTO KINDLY TAKEN AND PRESENTED BY MRS. CATHERINE WEED B. WARD.

cupboarded ways. He used to recall the red tiles dissolving into green with the weather stains over the stabling, the huge fireplace of the kitchen, the cumbrous locks and bolts, the watercress bed, the dogs' cemetery under yew and chestnut—the islet in the lake. We are inclined to think that Pater did not see any angels at Fish Hall. As we said, we thoroughly explored the place from cellar to roof, but we saw nothing larger than bats.

The neighbourhood consists of typical Kentish scenery. Our visit had been made after a week of heavy rains; the Medway had overflowed its meadows, and the long lines of disconsolate willows—'sallies," as they are locally called—stood knee deep in water. On the higher ground were hop gardens, with the disused poles stacked in pyramids, and here and there rose a picturesque circular oast-house, or place for the drying of hops, with its curious cowl. "I like the look of these oast houses," remarked a Kentish friend, "they give such an air of prosperity to a neighbourhood."

From Fish Hall we drove between tall hedges and Scotch firs to Hadlow, while before us, above the trees, soared the tall slim pinnacled tower of Hadlow Castle—170 feet high—reared by one of the Mays, Pater's kinsmen. Arrived at the village, we first strolled to the Castle, which is built in the Gothic style; has a great hall with a stained glass window representing the "Ascension;" and a long corridor. Surrounded with shrubs and picturesque trees, including several fine cedars of Lebanon, its appearance is attractive; still, it is of the Strawberry Hill style of building—showy, rather than substantial—and the name, "May's Folly," which the vulgar have bestowed upon it, will probably always cling.

9. Hadlow.

The church is in the Early English style, built of Kentish rag with a shingled tower.

G

On one of Pater's visits to Fish Hall he heard of an event that is still talked of in the neighbourhood. During a great flood, which covered the roads as well as the meadows, thirty hop-pickers, who were driving in a wagon through the water, were accidentally overturned at Hart Lake Bridge. Whether a wheel of the wagon caught against the bridge wall, or whether part of the bridge, damaged by the flood, gave way, or what really did happen, nobody knows, for not a soul was left to tell the tale. Recovered, one by one, from the turbid waters, the bodies, black and swollen, were borne to Hadlow churchyard, where an obelisk, raised by public subscription, still narrates the mournful tale. To another grave in Hadlow churchyard we shall have to refer in our seventh chapter.

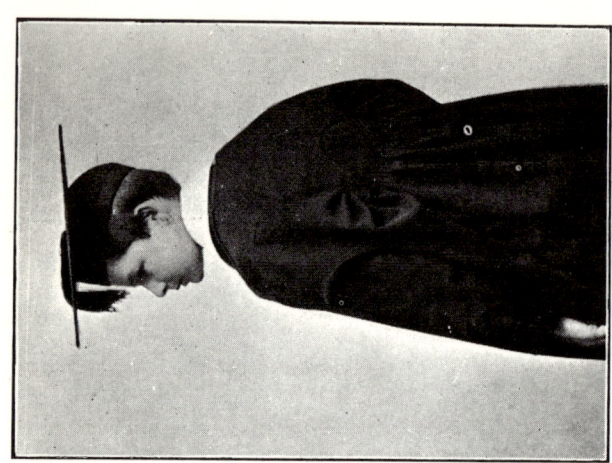

A KING'S SCHOOL BOY.
TO SHOW FRONT VIEW OF THE GOWN.

A KING'S SCHOOL BOY.
TO SHOW BACK VIEW OF THE GOWN.

CHAPTER IV

1853

PATER'S FIRST YEAR AT THE KING'S SCHOOL

When Walter was thirteen and a half it was decided to send him to the King's School, Canterbury; and, with this object in view, Mrs. Pater and Miss Elizabeth Pater removed to the village of Harbledown. Proceeding from Canterbury to Harbledown you ascend a hill, and on the left, near the entrance of the village, come upon a terrace of four white stuccoed narrow houses, "Harbledown Place," erected, as its lettering tells, in 1824; and the second from Canterbury was the home of the Paters. Mrs. Pater, "Aunt Bessie," and Walter, were all physically weak and often ailing, and the family had to contend not only against ill-health, but also against poverty—for their means were still, and long continued to be, very straitened. However, as is usually the case with those who fight bravely against untoward circumstances, they came off conquerors. Occasionally they had as guest their Aunt Bessie's cousin and bosom friend, Ann (daughter of John Church Pater), whom Walter, who became attached to her, afterwards visited at Liverpool; and we may notice that although twenty-eight years his senior—for she was born in 1810—she was to outlive him four years.[1]

As at Enfield, Walter was never without a cat, the white Angora of classic fame having been succeeded by a grey Persian, and we hear also of a white Persian, and of a cat that was coal black.

10. Harbledown.

[1] She died in September 1898, aged 88. She is buried at Weston Underwood, where there is a stone to her memory.

Few men can for the first time enter unmoved the hoary, ecclesiastical and storied city of Canterbury. It is no province of ours, however, to speak of its architectural glories save in so far as they concern Walter Pater. Imagine on the 2nd day of February—Candlemas morning—1853, a pensive, desolate, pallid, frightened, plain boy of thirteen accompanying his aunt—that "little crouched figure"—for she had taken him specially under her wing—down to Canterbury for the first time. Facing them all the way, and rising high above the roofs of the town is that crystallisation of poetry, the stately and wonderful Cathedral—the many-pinnacled pile that was to become the body of Pater's body just as his fleshly body encompassed his soul. This is no pretty idea of our own; the thought permeates all his writings. Life through, he was essentially a monk—sometimes an ascetic and painfully devout monk, sometimes a mocking, sceptical monk of the kind who painted on church walls frescoes of a character that excuse the sin of whitewash, and carved, on pillar capitals and misereres, libidinous centaurs and ægipans; but even when farthest from real religion Pater could never throw off—he never attempted to throw off—that body of his body. To return to the boy and his aunt making their way to Canterbury—now and again they pass an oast-house—here and there above the housetops rises some ancient battlemented pile or the pinnacled tower of some mediæval church with marvellous name—did he but know it—its meaning lost in the haze of antiquity. Windmills top the distant uplands. Arrived in Canterbury they turn sharply to the right at St. Dunstan's Church,[1] pass through the venerable and time-eaten West Gate, and so down the main thoroughfare of Canterbury between quaint houses with overhanging and threatening upper storeys, and gables with wood-

11. Canterbury.

---

[1] Later, Pater always used the footpath from Harbledown to Canterbury.

work and extraordinary cabalistic devices. This was more than fifty years ago, but even to-day Canterbury is like a leaf torn out of an illuminated missal; and you can think of nothing, as you pass through its streets, but aristocratic gentlemen in scarlet and miniver cloaks, or fantastic peacock-blue doublets, prodigal of sleeve, painfully tight yellow hose, and red shoes with toes too long to come entirely in the picture.

Turning to the left, the hunched lady and the boy are in Mercery Lane—the narrow thoroughfare in which the pilgrims to Becket's shrine used to lodge,[1] and purchase their necessaries—with a view of the Cathedral seen through the narrow slit formed by the bowing houses. They pass through the hoary and crumbling Christ Church gateway, with its maze of sculpture; and, lo! before them stands the Cathedral, with its forest of perpendicular lines, its airy towers, turrets, pinnacles, in all its majesty. A snowstorm had sprinkled the stupendous fane with white; big flakes were still falling, and it was vengeance cold. They are now in the Precincts. Taking the path that leads round Becket's crown (the extreme eastern portion of the Cathedral) they pass on their right an open space, called "The Oaks," from the rows of venerable trees that adorn it. In front of them extends a long house, "Canon Robert Moore's House," into the north wall of which was built the series of noble arches that formed part of the infirmary in the old monastic days. Canon Moore's house is now demolished, and the grey old arches stand out in all their venerable and ivy-festooned beauty. At this point we must suppose the travellers asked their way. Even now the tangle of ruins, arches, entries, and houses is bewildering enough to a stranger, and then it was even worse. Some one directs them to the east end of Canon Moore's. They pass between this spot and an old house called Meist Omers, or Master

[1] Some traces of the ancient inn, The Chequers of the Hope, mentioned by Chaucer, may still be seen in Mercery Lane.

Homers,⁽¹⁾ then the residence of the terrible Dr. Russell,⁽²⁾ formerly of Charterhouse—"the awful doctor" of *Pendennis* and Thackeray's letters—"Dr. Russell has been fierce to-day, yea, and full of anger."⁽³⁾ Even at Canterbury, where his power was weakened, boys dreaded his basilisk glance, and hurried past his door much as Christian did past the cave where "Giant Pope," "tho' grown so crazy and stiff in his joints," still glared frightfully, and gnawed his nails.

Next they thread an arched entrance, and proceed through the jitway between the back (that is the north) of Canon Moore's and the residence of Archdeacon Harrison. This brings them to the fearsome Dark Entry, which figures so conspicuously in the best known of the *Ingoldsby Legends*,⁽⁴⁾ the entry in which Nell Cook, with ashen face, deadly cold breath, and couched eyes, is said to stalk on Friday nights.

> And whoso in that entry dark doth feel that fatal breath,
> He ever dies within the year some dire untimely death.

Many tales are told of this lugubrious spot and those fearful Fridays. Indeed, the number of persons who have, or have not, seen Nell Cook must be enormous. Presently the travellers emerge into the spacious plot called the Green Court, where Walter probably saw, shuffling about, an elderly man carrying one of his legs straight, as if it were wooden, a character whom he was soon to know as "Old Norton," the school factotum— "the man with the leg." They pass the Deanery on their right, and approach the famous and beautiful Norman staircase which leads to the new King's School-

---

⁽¹⁾ Master Homer was an ecclesiastical lawyer of the Middle Ages.

⁽²⁾ John Russell 1787—1863.

⁽³⁾ Thackeray 14th February 1828.

⁽⁴⁾ Richard Barham, author of "The Ingoldsby Legends," was born at Canterbury in 1788. The work was published between 1840 and 1847.

REV. GEORGE WALLACE, M.A.,
HEAD MASTER OF THE KING'S SCHOOL, CANTERBURY.

From a sketch by Mr. L. L. Razé, the King's School Drawing Master, 1 February, 1848.

room, built in 1848, that is five years previous. They pass through one of the arches supporting the schoolroom, and find themselves in the "Mint Yard." On their left runs a weather-nibbled old building—the Almonry Chapel of the monks, used for many years as a schoolroom; in an angle formed by the almonry and a projection from it they notice the sweetstuff stall kept by Mrs. Norton, wife of "the man with the leg," and finally they reach their destination—the house of the Head Master—the Rev. George Wallace.

They are at the King's School—the school of Christopher Marlowe, William Harvey, and a whole galaxy of famous authors, bishops, deans, playwrights, statesmen, and other notabilities—the school of Dr. Strong in *David Copperfield*. At the door, we are certain that every vein and pulse in Pater's body trembled, but, whatever his fears, they were instantly dispelled at the sight of the stout, rotund, kindly figure of the Head Master, Mr. Wallace, who was getting into years, had "small, elephant eyes," a clean-shaven "blue face," and a bald crown, with a little dark hair above the ears. In religion he was a High Churchman, though to-day we should range him among the Moderates. Upright and conscientious, his aim, to use his own words, was to train up his pupils in sound learning, and in the true doctrines of the Church of England; and in wholesome discipline, to see his children walk in truth. Two maxims had fed his life, and he often put them before his pupils. 1. "Be content with a humble place at first, but spare no exertion to fit yourself for a higher." 2. "Regard your position in life as a revelation from God, who wills you to perform the duties assigned to it with a cheerful obedience." He made a favourable impression upon his pupils from the first; they regarded him with reverence and unaffected love, and in after years always spoke of him as "my dear old master."

12. The Rev. George Wallace.

Pater is informed that in summer his school hours will be—

              7 to 8.30
             10 to 1
             2.30 to 5;

in winter—

             9 to 1
             2.30 to 5.

So in the summer he would have to start from Harbledown at six. Matters having been adjusted with the Head Master, Miss Pater and Walter proceed to Palace Street, where, as he was to be a day boy, they make arrangements for his breakfasts and dinners—perhaps at Jackman the tailor's, where Walter, on becoming a King's Scholar, kept his gown.

The King's School is the oldest public school in England, having been founded in the 7th century—in those hazy days when Kent was a kingdom, and the arrival of Augustine's monks the latest sensation. Its history therefore is conterminous with that of the Cathedral itself. As time went on a great Benedictine monastery sprang up hard by, but the event of events was the murder of Thomas à Becket, whose shrine, as every one knows, became not only one of the wonders of this quarter of the world, but the object of countless pilgrimages. At the Reformation King Henry VIII., prompted by zeal for religion, seized the gold and jewels of Becket's shrine and the revenues of the monastery, and devoted them to his own use. He also reconstructed the school—the buildings of which had previously stood on the south side of the Cathedral—and placed it under the control of the Dean and Chapter, whence it has ever since been called after him, "The King's School." It is not, however, the only institution bearing Henry's name. That generous monarch gave away to various other persons and bodies a number of properties

13. The King's School.

REV. ANBY BEATSON.
SECOND MASTER AT THE KING'S SCHOOL.

DR. REINHOLD ROST.
GERMAN MASTER AT THE KING'S SCHOOL.

AT THE KING'S SCHOOL   43

that did not belong to him; and his memory has ever since, especially in University and Cathedral towns, been held not absolutely in abhorrence.

The school of Pater's boyhood differed materially from the institution of to-day. It is true that the principal buildings, as now, formed a quadrangle enclosing "the Mint Yard," but almost all were incredibly dilapidated; and the condition of the fittings and appointments corresponded. Those, indeed, who look at the beautiful buildings that to-day grace the quadrangle can form no idea whatever of their decrepit and frowsy predecessors; of the ramshackle staircases, gaping floors, cracked doors, black, knife-marked desks, broken and dirty ceilings of Walter Pater's time. One building, and one only, had adopted its present appearance, namely, the fine new schoolroom over the Norman arches.

The south side of the Mint Yard, we said, was occupied by the old Almonry Chapel, converted into a schoolroom; [1] and in Pater's time both that and the new schoolroom were used for teaching. The pupils first assembled in the new school by way of the Norman staircase, after which the English and German classes crossed the Mint Yard to the Almonry Chapel, and the Sixth Form filed into a class-room situated on the east side of the Mint Yard.

Walter Pater, as we said, was admitted on 3rd February, 1853, among other new-comers on the same day being George Collard—now Sir George, and Mayor of Canterbury.[2] The boys of the King's School were either "scholars" or "commoners." The former, who wore a black gown, with long inverted cones of cloth, known in the school as "jelly bags," and a square cap,

---

[1] It was demolished in 1865, that is seven years after Pater left.

[2] The Register containing their names is inscribed "This book was given to the King's School in the Cathedral of Christ's Church, Canterbury, for containing a register of admissions, and an account of benefactions, by me
Osmund Beauvoir
Head Master 1750—1782

with a black tassel,[1] were fifty in number; and we may notice that fifty youths served Monseigneur in *Gaston de Latour,* which indeed contains not a few reminiscences of the King's School. The Commoners had, and still have, no distinguishing dress. Although entered on 3rd February, 1853, it is probable that Pater was not elected a King's Scholar until December, 1853.[2]

At any rate, after that date he was to be seen in his black gown and cap with black tassel; or on a saint's day, or other occasion when church was attended, in a fine white flowing surplice. There were then about a hundred boys in all, and seven masters; now there are 250 boys and twenty masters.

The assistant masters in Pater's time were Mr. Anby Beatson, M.A., Rev. Philip Menzies Sankey, B.A., Mr. Fisher (English and Writing), Monsieur Martinet (French), Herr Rost (German), and Monsieur Rasé (Drawing). Mr. Anby Beatson, the second master, who lived at the north-west corner of the Mint Yard, was a portly, comfortable, impassive, slightly satirical old man, "with a face like a moon, and a stately gait." The boys—and all loved him—called him "Toe-y," there being a tradition in the school that at one time he used to pronounce the word "to" "toe"; but Pater always alluded to him as "Ab," after the initials A.B. Between his house and that of Mr. Wallace stood a house occupied by Mr. Jones, the Cathedral organist, a

14. The Assistant Masters.

---

[1] Not a purple tassel as in *Emerald Uthwart.* Boys of the first two classes now wear gowns of black cloth cut in much the same shape as those worn by the scholars at Westminster. The senior scholars wear black gowns of mohair in shape closely resembling those worn by scholars on the foundation of an Oxford College. In Walter Pater's time these three distinct classes did not exist.

[2] The papers extant refer only to an election in December of each year—not in July and December as now: and the List for December 1852, which is preserved, does not contain Pater's name. The School Register also gives 1853 (no month) as the date when he became a King's Scholar.

THE HOME OF THE PATER FAMILY
AT HARBLEDOWN, NEAR CANTERBURY.

gentleman who once declared that he had seen Nell Cook. The boys naturally expected of him that he would die the same year, and, as he did not die, they thought it very shabby of him (as, of course, it was), and he never after entirely regained their respect.

Mr. Sankey, the third master, was a generation younger than Mr. Wallace and Mr. Beatson; but we are most interested in the tall, portly, weather-beaten, red complexioned, clean-shaven, broad-shouldered Mr. Fisher, for it was from him that Pater first derived his taste for the best things in literature. Old, antiquated, and poor, Mr. Fisher looked in his black coat and check trousers "not unlike a character of Dickens drawn (favourably) by Phiz," and a striking contrast to the well-liking and robed masters Wallace, Beatson, and Sankey. His duty was to look over the boys' "themes," to hear them read Shakespeare, and to prepare the portions for recitation on speech days; but not only did he teach English literature, he was himself "a choice litterateur."

Dr. Reinhold Rost,[1] the German master, resided at St. Augustine's College. He was already, though but a little over thirty, familiar with all the leading languages of Europe and the nearer East, being surpassed as a linguist by no man of his day, with the exception of his friend, Sir Richard Burton. Teaching tiresome schoolboys who had no appetite for languages, was naturally distasteful to him, but he had one sympathetic pupil, a tall, good-looking lad named W. K. W. Chafy.[2] Chafy, however, revelled not only in the German language and literature, but also in heraldry; and owing to his familiarity with the three choughs that strut in the arms of the city, and with

[1] Dr. Rost (1822—1896) first taught at King's School in 1847. From 1863 to 1869 he was secretary to the Royal Asiatic Society, and in the latter year he became librarian at the India Office. He died at Canterbury in 1896.

[2] Now the Rev. Dr. Chafy, of Rous Lench Court. His father lived at Charlton Park, four miles from Canterbury.

griffin, wyvern, hippogriff, and other alarming cattle, his schoolfellows spoke of him respectfully as a sort of Garter King of Arms.

Of M. Razé, the drawing master, many memorials are still to be found in Canterbury, in the shape of portraits of the leading inhabitants, and prints of the Green Court and the school buildings—the lithographs of the Rev. George Wallace and the Interior of the Chapter House on Speech Day, reproduced in this book being from his facile pencil. Most of the masters, as we have seen, were old and timeworn, like the school buildings. Indeed, there was antiquity everywhere—the very rooks whose nests rocked in the trees of the Mint Yard seeming venerable, and, in Pater's phrase, "a little weary."

THE KING'S SCHOOL, CANTERBURY.—THE SCHOOL HOUSE.

CHAPTER V

SCHOOL ANECDOTES

Walter Pater had entered upon school life, and he did not like it; yet his first fortnight at Canterbury was paradise compared with the second, for towards the end of February very severe weather again set in. Pater had no sympathy with the sports of the other boys, and in the great snowball fights that took place in the Mint Yard and round the Norman staircase between the King's School boys and the town "cads," he could see neither enjoyment nor sense. While others were dashing about with torn clothes and glowing cheeks he preferred to stand sheltered and undamaged in a corner with shivering frame and blue nose. But his schoolfellows did not leave him long in peace. Being a newcomer and not very strong he was soon called upon to join with others of his calibre in making pyramids of snowballs for the big boys to throw. Both enemies and friends hustled and pelted him—the enemy because he was a King's School Boy, his friends because he did not make snowballs fast enough, and the shouts which the frenzied antagonists uttered to hearten one another were to him more terrifying than the whoops of Red Indians. He did not care whether the town was driven pell-mell back into Palace Street or the school was forced ignominiously into Green Court. All he required was shelter, whether behind Beatson, the prodigiously fat son of the second master, or on the Norman Staircase—a frequent refuge, where, when he could, he watched the battle between its miniature columns—

15. The Snow Fights.

fervently praying all the while for a thaw; and to his dying day he remembered these scenes with disgust and hatred. At all times of the year the Norman Staircase served as a screen for pugilistic encounters, many a stubborn fight taking place in the corner behind it. But Pater never fought. He said he did not seem to want a black eye. Nor was he ambitious to get above the roof of the staircase, and bestraddle the ridge—a feat which every other boy hoped to perform some time or other before leaving. Indeed, he looked upon his schoolfellows as a pack of brutal, irreconcilable savages, and they upon him as a hopeless milksop.

If he regarded snowballing as an imbecile amusement, another pastime of the boys of the King's School gave him even more disgust—namely the custom of keeping snakes, usually vipers —uncanny creatures about a foot long, marked with dark lozenges—which were accommodated with long narrow cages fronted with wires. Sometimes the boys themselves caught them, but as a rule they bought them from Hawkins, the Sexton—"Viper George" as he was called—who used to go searching for them with a forked stick, his favourite hunting-ground being "White Hall Bank," near the White Hall public-house, and the railway between Harbledown and Thanington. After removing the fangs, Viper George would bring the vermin down to the Mint Yard and turn them out in a livid writhing heap on the pavement. Every boy knew all about vipers—of their habit of flying at scarlet cloth; of their weakness for swallowing their young and presently disgorging them all alive; of the oil obtained from them and its value for bites and bruises. One day at Harbledown William Pater, conversant with his brother's antipathy to these creatures, mischievously twisted a viper round the handle of a door, and Walter, who did not notice the horror until he had clasped it, nearly died of fright. When, in after years he came to write *Marius the*

16. Snakes.

THE KING'S SCHOOL, CANTERBURY.—THE MINT YARD.

Epicurean—and Marius's horror of snakes [1] will be remembered—no incident of his boyhood stood out more sharply; and we may at once say that that story has a purely English setting, just as Keats's gods and goddesses disported themselves pleasantly among the daisies, the box trees and the yews of the Isle of Wight and Dorking; and when still later he applied himself seriously to the study of Dante's "Inferno" he found none of the scenes more horrible than those in which serpents are introduced.

The masters, we said, were popular, but still more popular were two Newfoundland dogs, Tip and Nep, who belonged respectively to Mr. Wallace and Mr. Beatson. The masters taught the boys, and the boys in return taught the dogs—Tip, in particular, being quick to learn any piece of wickedness. Dotted about the Green Court were posts, placed to defend the grass, and when one of them showed signs of weakness it was pointed out to Tip, who at once set about scratching away the soil with his paws until the right depth was reached, when he would vigorously attack the selected spot with his teeth, biting out pieces of the wood, and persevering until the weakened post snapped asunder. If time did not permit the work of destruction to be completed the soil was put back and the attack renewed the first opportunity. Nep often assisted, and the dogs enjoyed the mischief as much as the boys.

17. Tip and Nep.

In these sports Pater never joined, though with his keen sense of humour, he must often have laughed heartily at them. His chief delight was to roam solitarily about the Precincts—and the boys seem to have been allowed to go just where they liked—among the old arches, in the cloisters with their hollow and dismal echoes, down gloomy entries where dark spirits stalked, and in dank and earthy vaults—for indeed he was far less afraid of the uneasy dead than of the happy living.

[1] *Marius*, Vol. I., pp. 23 and 24.

We have already alluded to that important institution, Mrs. Norton's Stall, which stood in the corner formed by the old school and a projection from it. Mrs. Norton was a stout good-humoured body, and on the stall among the sweets, tarts and cakes lay always a big slate covered with boys' names and the following signs O, ᴏ, /, ,, meaning respectively a shilling, a sixpence, a penny, and a halfpenny, though the boys called them moons, half-moons, longs and shorts. It was against the rules to give any boys credit, but there were few who did not obtain it. In many cases, indeed, the next term's allowance was heavily mortgaged, so that when a boy once ran into debt he usually remained in debt to the end. Hungry but prudent boys with perhaps 3d. or 4d. in ready money to spend would lurk about the bun and tart tray for a quarter of an hour before deciding how to lay it out; while another reckless boy, perhaps already in debt, further credit having been refused, would rush in, suddenly stick his finger through a tart and say, "Missis, how much for that damaged tart?" Mrs. Norton, very indignant, would reply, "Really, Master ——, you are too bad, I shall tell Mr. ——" (naming one of the monitors). Then she would add, "No one will eat it after your finger has been through, so you had better take it, and I'll put it down." Mrs. Norton's husband, who has already been mentioned, was also one of the "characters" of the Precincts. He mowed the grass in the Green Court, and assisted the heavy roller in getting the ground ready for a cricket match—acting as shaft horse. As we noticed, he carried one of his legs straight as if it were wooden. This was owing to a stiff knee joint; and when he was acting as shaft horse, it was considered great fun to put on plenty of power and push the roller along, driving Norton with it at a rate which rendered it difficult for him to manage his stiff leg—a proceeding which put the old man into a violent temper, and caused him to use language which

18 Mrs. Norton's Stall.

THE KING'S SCHOOL, CANTERBURY.—NORMAN STAIRCASE TO THE SCHOOLROOM.

would not have been approved of by the Dean and Chapter. To return to Mrs. Norton, for long she enjoyed a monopoly as seller of sweets and cakes, but the dragon Envy managed to invade even those quiet Precincts, and one day Mr. Teal, a cathedral verger, who lived in a house on the west side of the Green Court, set up a rival tuck-shop, wholly to Mrs. Norton's indignation. The boys, however, chivalrously took her part, with the result that within a fortnight Mr. Teal had to close his shutters; and, ever after, it was considered the correct thing when passing to accost him with—

> Good morning, Mister Teal,
> I hope you feel quite weel,

a greeting which he invariably accepted with a silent but contemptuous lip.

The opening day of cricket was usually the first Monday in May, on which occasion a whole holiday was granted to the school. The bathing season was also supposed to commence at that time—the favourite resort being a spot *19. Boating.* just outside the city called Bingley's Island, but even bathing was less popular among the boys than boating. Though Pater had an ambition to learn to row, he could never at Canterbury be prevailed upon to adventure himself on the water; but he daringly determined if ever he came across a very small, very quiet and very shallow pond with a well-tested boat on it, to try his skill, be the consequences what they might; and, as we shall see, he kept his word. The boats on the river being few, and most of them heavy tubs, the boys used to make up parties; and a race always took place for certain craft, one called "The Fly" being the favourite. It was no uncommon event to arrive at the spot and find "The Fly" just put off into the stream with the crew that had secured her, and if those in "The Fly" jeered (as they usually did) at those who were too late, a reply was sure to be made with stones or pieces of turf by the land party, who would then hire, and try to content themselves with, some other old tub of heavier build.

The Dean of Canterbury was the paralytic Very Rev. W. Rowe Lyall, brother to the Rector of Harbledown, the Vice-Dean being the Venerable Benjamin Harrison [1]—who was virtually Regent of the Cathedral during Dean Lyall's incapacity—a small, thin man with a high, large nose, "hooked," says one who remembers that fine feature, "like a gollywog's," and a cast in one eye.

20. Arthur Penrhyn Stanley.

There were six canons, the senior being the Rev. Robert Moore,[2] a notorious pluralist, "who had the most charming silvery voice you could imagine, and read beautifully;" the second Archdeacon Croft,[3] also a pluralist—"a splendid old man whose sermons were well-turned little essays;" the third, the stern and terrible Doctor Russell; the fourth, Archdeacon Harrison; the fifth the Rev. A. P. Stanley,[4] afterwards Dean of Westminster, whom Pater called "Aps," after his initials; the sixth Canon Stone; and all had fine carriages, spanking horses and powdered men-servants, and made a prodigious display both at home and abroad. The Canon-in-Residence read the lessons on Sundays, and it was the duty of the monitors of the King's School to go in turn to the Chapter Vestry and present to him a list of absentees. Of the six canons the one whom Pater liked the best was Stanley, who had come to Canterbury—had made his "first great flight from Oxford"—on a dreary day in November, 1851. The mannikin—for he was absurdly small—told his friends

---

[1] His wife, I believe, was daughter of Henry Thornton, of Clapham.

[2] Son of Archbishop Moore, who died in 1804.

[3] His house was at the south-west corner of the Green Court.

[4] He resided in the house between Master Homer's and the Deanery.

THE KING'S SCHOOL, CANTERBURY.—FROM THE GREEN COURT.

to think of him as "lost in the huge cathedral," and he took such short tripping steps, and walked so fast in his long surplice to his seat in the choir that Pater likened him to a mouse running along. But if he was little, every ounce, or so those who loved him said, was sound and good. Always impressed by historical associations, Stanley was at once riveted by those of Canterbury. To no other modern had Augustine, Becket and the Black Prince appeared so real. Previous to his arrival at Canterbury these worthies had been impalpable shades, but before twelve months had passed —so much did he talk, lecture and sermonize upon them —they once more stood revealed in flesh and blood, mail and mitre. You might meet them under any threatening arch or leering gargoyle. Again Augustine held aloft his wooden cross, again the Black Prince filled his cup at the Harbledown well that takes his name, again his corpse was borne with sepulchral pomp into the mourning Cathedral—"four black banners following;" while "the holy blisful martir" [1] died yearly on 29th December "in the twilight." His shrine, for those who had eyes to see, again blinded with its gems and gorgeous glare of gold; again eager and dusty pilgrims bustled in Mercery Lane and the Chequer of the Hope. A little later Stanley himself turned pilgrim—the object of his journey being the Holy Land; and, after his return, his sermons and lectures bristled with impressions and recollections Oriental, while among his many hearers none listened with more rapt attention than Walter Pater, who all but idolized his microscopic but eloquent palmer.

[1] Chaucer.

CHAPTER VI

IN THE CATHEDRAL

Far more to Pater's taste than bathing, or even than watching the boats were the ceremonies on Saints' Days, when the boys, as on Sundays, marched in procession to the Cathedral; and his only regret was that of these days the Church of England recognised so few. One of my visits to Canterbury happened to be on the Festival of Saint Simon and Saint Jude, and I had the pleasure of seeing the procession, which had formed up by the Norman Staircase, making its way under the lime trees on the west side of the Green Court to the Cathedral. At its head were the fifty King's Scholars in their long white surplices and college caps—the two senior boys leading. Then followed the Commoners, accompanied here and there by a white-robed monitor, and lastly the masters in their University robes. In was an impressive sight—a sight such as Archbishop Cranmer himself, over three hundred and fifty years ago, may have often witnessed, though on the other side of the Cathedral; for we know that as the first visitor of the reconstituted "Free Schoole within the Cimitery" he took a personal interest in the election of the King's Scholars. Queen Elizabeth saw it too, when, on her famous visit to Canterbury in 1574, the head boy of the school stood forward at the great west doorway of the Cathedral and welcomed Her Majesty in a Latin oration. Even Becket, Canterbury's most famous ecclesiastic, may have watched a similar, though unsurpliced, procession wending its way to the Cathedral from the ancient school of the Archbishop; for in these venerable foun-

21 A Saint's Day.

dations customs change even less than human nature, or than the ancient and perpetual rooks that squabble on the tree tops or strut below on the rich turf. In Pater's day the procession, after arriving at the south-west corner of the Green Court, and the house that used to be the Cellarer's Lodging,[1] threaded the old archway through which the supplies used to be brought into the kitchen of the monastery, and then ascended the flight of stone steps through the remains of the large monastic dormitory built by Lanfranc in 1080. Then turning abruptly to the left it went through a passage built by Lanfranc to connect the dormitory [2] with the choir; and after another sharp turn, this time to the right, it entered the North Choir Transept, close to where the memorial tomb of Archbishop Tait now stands, and finally entered the choir near the elaborately decorated tomb of Archbishop Chicheley. The scholars took their seats close under the stalls occupied by the Dean and Residentiary Canons, while "the commoners had their own places nearer the Archbishop's throne." I enter the choir—"the melodious mellow-lighted space always," to use Pater's words, "three days behind the temperature outside." It is a dun, gray morning, and I am reminded of Pater's appetite for dimness, and the soft, subdued colouring in which he loves to picture the great minster where Emerald Uthwart came to worship with his schoolmates—"The choir, to which they glide in order to their places below the clergy, seems conspicuously cold and sad. But the empty chapels lying beyond it all about into the distance are a trap on sunny mornings for the clouds of yellow effulgence. The Angel Steeple is a lantern within, and sheds down a flood of the like just beyond the gates. Here, to boyish sense, one seems diminished to nothing at all, amid the

[1] Now the Bishop of Dover's house, known as Chillenden Chambers.

[2] The site is now partly a lawn and partly occupied by the Chapter Library.

grand waves, wave upon wave, of patiently wrought stone; the daring height, the daring severity of the innumerable long, upward ruled lines, rigidly bent just at last, in due place, into the reserved grace of the perfect Gothic arch."

While I am musing a clear "Amen" comes from the vestry in St. Andrew's Chapel, and the procession enters. I am sitting in the stalls, so it advances in my direction. The choristers, in their surplices and purple cassocks, are leading. Then follow the lay clerks; a black-robed verger with his long silver staff; the minor canons and other of the Cathedral clergy; another verger bearing a staff; and then the Dean. Next come the King's Scholars, two and two, preceding the Head Master and the Senior Assistant Master, who close the long array of surpliced members of the Cathedral foundation. Behind them come the commoners, juniors leading; and last of all the assistant masters, who take their places in the stalls. I observe that two of the senior King's Scholars, when they reach the Litany desk in the centre of the choir, turn about and stand facing eastward, watching the commoners as one after another they file into their places; nor until every boy and master has reached his seat do the two "watchers," as they are called, move away to join the rows of scholars.[1]

The service begins. It is choral, and the singing has a grace, a dignified beauty worthy of this our greatest English Cathedral. The Dean walks from his place in the stalls to the lectern, his own verger preceding him with the silver wand, and when the lesson is read he is once more conducted by the verger to his stall. There is more singing, then prayers. It is the service of the Church of England, but everything is so strange, so shadowy. There is a cough. One is awakened as if from a dream, and sees the long lines of boys kneeling —as the Benedictine monks and novices might have

[1] In Pater's time the choir and the clergy came in some minutes after the King's School boys.

THE GREEN COURT, CANTERBURY.

knelt beneath that very roof-tree more than five hundred years ago. Again one realises as never before, something of what Pater felt when he wrote, "The very place one is in, its stone-work, its empty spaces, invade you; seem to question you masterfully as to your purpose in being here at all, amid the great memories of the past of this school."

The service is concluded. The choristers lead the way and the long procession—scholars, commoners, masters—meanders back through corridor and court to the school again.

In Pater's time, in compliance with an old statute of the Cathedral—the clergy on entering the choir, bowed towards the Dean's stall.[1] A story is told of one minor canon who disliked this custom and refusing to observe it was threatened with deprivation. So being obliged to conform, he always bowed to the ground in a very ridiculous manner, and whenever he met the Dean or a canon in the street did the same, saying "Good day, my worthy master." The Chapter finding him (as a wag) very troublesome gave him a fat living in Norfolk, and thus were quit of him. After the presentation and before he left Canterbury, happening to meet Miss Hester S——, one of a clever Mint Yard family, on her way to service, he cried, "What, going to the Puppet Show, Miss Hester?" "No," replied Miss S——, "that exhibition has ceased; Punch is ordered into Norfolk."

The behaviour of some of Pater's schoolfellows, and especially of a brilliant and audacious lad named B——n, during the Cathedral services was often censurable, but, curiously enough, nobody seems to have noticed it except Pater and the other boys who stood near.

Among the King's Scholars was an idle, clever boy named Pye. One day while he stood squinting through a hole in one of the ramshackle doors of the school premises, and jibing at a boy on the opposite side, the

[1] That is before the words "When the wicked man," &c.

latter having thrust his hand through a lower hole seized Pye's necktie, pulled with all his might, and nearly strangled his victim, who was rescued only just in time. B——n, an accomplished mimic, stood next to Pye at the Cathedral services; and in the Benedicite, after this event, he used to set out a throat and sing lustily, imitating Archdeacon Harrison's high, clear and solemn voice—

"Oh, all ye strangled Pyes, bless ye the Lord."

His voice, too, was always the loudest on the last Sunday of every half-year, when it was the custom of the boys to shout, with exceptional lung, the final "Amen." There is a reference to B——n's levity in *Gaston de Latour,* where one of Gaston's companions is represented as singing with truly mediæval licence to the sacred music those songs from the streets which were really in their hearts. As for Pater himself, he may be said to have really lived only when he was in church. His ecstasy, indeed, during these services reached an exaltation comparable only to that of impassioned saints and martyrs.

To return to B——n, this boy was in the habit of making in Archdeacon Harrison's voice all sorts of absurd speeches, both in school and out of it. After these sallies, while the boys round him were ready to die of laughter, he would observe gravely, still imitating the Archdeacon, "Don't laugh, dear boys, or you'll commit f*****ation."

Of the glories of the Cathedral the most fascinating is perhaps the Bell Harry Tower—the Angel Steeple as it was also called, from the angel that originally surmounted it, and as Pater himself calls it in "Emerald Uthwart."

22. The Bell Harry Tower.

In the centre of the lantern of this tower is a circular aperture, and Pater must have heard, and have listened with breathless interest to the story connected with it. In the chamber above there was a windlass

THE PROCESSION TO THE CATHEDRAL.

"On Saturday half-holidays the scholars are taken to church in their surplices across the court, under the lime trees."—*Emerald Uthwart.*

for drawing up rolls of lead or other materials for repairing the higher parts of the tower or the roof of the Cathedral. The windlass was managed by a deaf workman, who was stationed in the upper chamber. When the workmen below brought in any load and had fastened it, they pulled the rope as a signal, and he began to turn. One day a vestryman standing in the Martyrdom,[1] and happening to look upwards, saw, to his horror, a boy, holding to a rope, rise above the organ, which was then on the screen. Thinking this some boyish freak, yet breathless for the consequences, he hastened to the spot. His terror increased when he saw the boy nearly at the top, and then saw him let down. He did come down in safety, but with hands terribly lacerated, and he was almost lifeless from pain and fright. It transpired that this boy, a King's Scholar, coming into the Cathedral, had seen the pendent rope, and had taken hold of it and pulled it, with the result that the man above began to draw him up. The boy thought it was fun, and that the man would raise him only a few yards and then let him down. However, he soon found that he was being gradually drawn to the top, so held on with the grimness of desperation. When the deaf man at last grasped the situation, instead of landing him, he, immediately, in terror for the boy, began to wind the rope back, and let him down, thus doubling the danger; but wonderful to say, the boy, though ready to drop from exhaustion, finally, as we said, reached the ground in safety, and little the worse for his frightful experience. Few King's School boys could pass under the Bell Harry Tower without recalling the incident, and some would shudder as the vivid picture presented itself of the wretched schoolboy dangling in space.

[1] The place, of course, where Becket was murdered.

CHAPTER VII

JANUARY 1854 TO DECEMBER 1854

THE DEATH OF PATER'S MOTHER

Pater, who was now a King's Scholar, in cap, gown, and "jellybag," had scarcely resumed school in the year 1854, when he lost his mother. Her health, as we have seen, had for some time been failing, but when, in January, she went on a visit to Fish Hall, there seemed no special cause for uneasiness. Just before she started, an event occurred which Pater never after called to mind without self-reproach. To use his own words in *Marius* [1] "it happened that, through some sudden incomprehensible petulance there had been an angry childish gesture, and a slighting word, at the very moment of her departure, actually for the last time." This is the more noticeable in that Pater had one of the sweetest of tempers, and apparently lost control of himself not more than three or four times in the course of his life. Mrs. Pater died at Fish Hall on 25th February, 1854, and was buried at Hadlow Church, distant, as we have seen, about two miles; and when the news of her death came to Walter, he thought, to use his own words, of that "marred parting" with "peculiar bitterness." Her tombstone, which has a simple Gothic head, stands at the S.W. corner of the

23. Death of his Mother, 5th Feb., 1854.

---

[1] Vol. I., p. 41. I have proof that this is autobiographical.

GRAVE OF PATER'S MOTHER.

FROM A PHOTO KINDLY TAKEN AND PRESENTED BY MRS. CATHERINE W. WARD.

churchyard; and its inscription, cut in clear letters, runs:—

> SACRED
> To the Memory of
> MARIA,
> Widow of the late
> RICHARD   PATER,   ESQ.,
> Surgeon, of London.
> Who died the 25th February, 1854,
> Aged 53 Years.
> Leaving a family to sorrow
> for her loss.

It appears to have been in this year that Pater paid his visit to Hursley in Hampshire, where he had the privilege of meeting Keble. At any rate it certainly took place before February, 1855. Of Keble's achievements as a poet (*The Christian Year* had appeared in 1827); and of the principal events in the great High Church movement inaugurated by Keble, Pusey and Newman, including the issue of *The Tracts for the Times,* and the secession of Newman to Rome (1845), Pater, though only a boy of fifteen, was perfectly aware. Indeed, these events had appealed to him, perhaps more than to his adult friends. Keble had been settled at Hursley some twenty years, and the charm of his manner and the saintliness of his character excited the love and reverence of all who met him. He was then about 62, a spare man rather below the middle-size, with grey hair and few front teeth. His books and pictures alone would have revealed his character. Over the fireplace in his dining-room hung an engraving of Domenichino's St. John; in his study was Westmacott's marble bust of Newman; while the place of honour on his shelves was occupied by Pearson, Butler and Hooker, whom he he called "our three English classics."

24. Hursley and Keble, about 1854.

"At Evening Prayer every one stood while Mr. Keble read six or eight verses from the Scriptures, and then the servants and all kneeled down, not at chairs, nor at a table, but without support."

Pater and Keble took walks together by the Norman moat in the adjoining park, and conversed also in Keble's study; and while Keble was attracted by his companion's pensive seriousness, Pater never forgot Keble's benign face, or even his personal peculiarities. He imitated Keble in the way of holding a book, and there is a reference to this in "Emerald Uthwart." [1] "'He holds his book in a peculiar way,' notes in manuscript one of his tutors, 'holds on to it with both hands.'" Many years after, seeing Mr. Edmund Gosse take up a book, Pater said to him, "You are holding that book just Keble's way." This visit proved a great quickener to Pater's religious aspirations; he liked in after years to talk about it; he introduced Keble as the "saintly person who loved him tenderly" into *The Child in the House*; [2] and one of his poems [3] as we shall presently see, was coloured by recollections of a verse in *The Christian Year*. Apparently Pater never again met Keble, who died 29th March, 1866; at any rate, we have no record of a second meeting.

In February, 1854, there entered the school a lad of solemn countenance and slightly saturnine disposition, named Henry Dombrain, son of Mr. William Dombrain, [4] hop grower and wine merchant, of Canterbury—a gentleman of Huguenot descent whose ancestors were said to have come over at the time of the persecutions in an open boat. A good-hearted but curiously narrow-minded boy, Dombrain—"Archdeacon Dombrain," as the other boys called him—was a very Procrustes for expecting everybody else to conform to rules of which he himself approved; but he and Pater presently

25. Henry Dombrain, Feb. 1854

---

[1] *Miscellaneous Studies*, p. 196.
[2] *Miscellaneous Studies*, p. 166.
[3] "The Fan of Fire." She Chapter XV.
[4] One branch of the family spelt the name D'Ombrain. Sir James D'Ombrain, an uncle of Henry Dombrain's, died in 1871, and is buried in Canterbury Cathedral, where there is a brass to his memory.

DEATH OF PATER'S MOTHER

became bosom friends, and it was from the Dombrains that Pater obtained some of the material which he used many years after in his story of the Huguenot persecution—*Gaston de Latour*. The Dombrains, who lived in an ugly house in St. Margaret's Street, attended St. Margaret's Church, of which the Rev. Edward Harrison Woodall, an advanced Ritualist with distinct leanings towards Catholicism, was rector.[1] Mr. Woodall took a sincere interest in Henry Dombrain, and assisted him in his studies, while Pater also came under Mr. Woodall's influence, and gradually adopted his religious views.

There were originally two great days at the school, namely, the Festival of the Ascension and School Feast Day, the latter being usually in September and on a Thursday. On Ascension Day, after morning service, the three senior boys, standing at the Head Master's desk, used to recite, before the Dean and Canons, speeches selected from Livy or Quintus Curtius, after which the Dean would say a few words of commendation and request a holiday from that hour till afternoon service on the Saturday. In Pater's time, however, the custom of giving so long a holiday had been discontinued, and the day was unnoticed except by attendance at the morning service in the Cathedral and a half-holiday in the afternoon. School Feast Day, however, grew in importance every year, and a number of the Reports of the Proceedings of "The School Feast Society" have been preserved, including that for 28th September, 1854, the second in which Pater took part.

26. School Speech Day, 28th Sept., 1854.

A short time before the great day, rehearsals were held in the Chapter House, where the proceedings always took place; and this was the signal for the preparation of darts—made of pieces of stick with a pen nib at one end and a paper tail at the other. The more daring boys used to steal into the Chapter House before

[1] He went over to Rome in 1859. See Chapter XXII.

the time and amuse themselves by throwing the darts at the roof, which is of great height, in the hope that they would stick—a result never accomplished, it is said, except by one boy whose missile kept its proud place for many years. On the great day everybody put on Sunday dress and looked on good terms with himself. Even old Norton and his straight leg were adorned for the occasion, and Tip and Nep wore favours. Old feuds were forgotten. Everybody was amiable to everybody—even to the mercenary Mr. Teal, who on this one day in the year was allowed to go by without the rhythmical address respecting his health. A procession was made to the Cathedral by the route already described, the preacher on this occasion being the Rev. Thomas Castle Southey, and after the sermon the masters and pupils proceeded to the Chapter House. A platform was extemporized, and between that and a table loaded with prizes sat Mr. Wallace in gown and bands, beaming with smiles. On the other side of the platform sat Mr. Beatson "like a moon at the full," and in front of it were the Dean and Canons; while the rest of the space was occupied by relations and friends. One boy after another mounted the steps to deliver his speech or recitation, and then the prizes were given away, the boy who this year most distinguished himself being Henry B. Biron.[1] Pater is not mentioned, but Dombrain, who was in Form 2, obtained a prize for classics. Mr. Wallace, in magniloquent language, addressed a special speech to each boy as he handed the prize, and the hero, after thanking him, made a ceremonious bow to the Dean and Chapter before resuming his seat. These numerous little speeches by Mr. Wallace were perfect marvels for the variety of their matter and their wealth of quotation. But then they were the result of much study, for the good but astute old gentleman got them off by heart some days before the event, and placed copies in the hands of the reporters

---

[1] Now Vicar of Lympne, Hythe.

A SPEECH DAY IN THE CHAPTER HOUSE, CANTERBURY.

From a Sketch by L. L. Razé, Drawing Master at the King's School.

of the local papers; and the amusing feature about it all was that the reporters did not keep their counsel. However, the proceedings were invariably pleasant. Boys blushed under the weight of the numerous unsuspected virtues that Mr. Wallace discovered in them; Dean and Canons made complimentary remarks as the heroes passed them—even the terrible Dr. Russell mellowing; mothers rose into the seventh heaven; uncles and other relations who had attended on previous occasions winked at each other; and the reporters, who had already the whole of the speeches in print in their pockets, scribbled down nothing at all like mad.

CHAPTER VIII

JANUARY 1855 TO DECEMBER 1855

JOHN RAINIER MCQUEEN

On February 6th, 1855, among the new day scholars at the King's School were two brothers named McQueen —John Rainier and Robert [1]—great grandsons of Robert McQueen, Lord Braxfield, the original of Robert Louis Stevenson's Weir of Hermiston.[2] On their mother's side they were descended from a noble Huguenot family of Poitou named Rainier, one of whom was a member of an embassy to England in the time of Henry VIII. John Rainier McQueen, who was eight months younger than Pater, and Robert McQueen, who was three years younger, had indeed precisely such ancestors as Pater considered a boy should have. Their father, Colonel (afterwards General McQueen late of the 15th Hussars, a smart, handsome man with a touch of the dandy, who made a gorgeous appearance in stripes and gold lace, had in the autumn of 1854, after the proclamation of war with Russia,[3] been appointed to command the Depôts in Canterbury; and he resided in the south-eastern suburb called Barton Fields.[4] In those days there was much coming and going of soldiery in the city. "If you stole out of an evening," says Pater,[5]

27. John Rainier McQueen, 6th Feb., 1855.

[1] He died in 1887. Mr. J. R. McQueen is now of Braxfield, Lanarkshire.

[2] See *Weir of Hermiston*, Editorial Note, p. 275. The vivid scenes between the Lord Advocate and Mrs. Weir will be remembered. The wives of Scotch justices do not take the title of "Lady." Lord Braxfield was not of so mean an origin as Weir of Hermiston, for his father was the owner of Braxfield (an estate near Lanark).

[3] War was proclaimed 28th March 1854.

[4] No. 3, Barton Fields.

[5] *Emerald Uthwart*.

his school days, and is possibly traceable (though we would not labour the point) to his intimacy with McQueen. We may even go so far as to say that Pater's only claim to fame, apart from his striking style, depends upon his series of Imaginary Portraits; for only those of his works are of real value that embrace these sketches. No man cares a peppercorn for his studies of French Churches, while his *Plato and Platonism* and the second half of *Greek Studies,* which deals only with sculpture, fall leagues below the pictures of the immortal Denys l'Auxerrois and his equally airy brethren. For the present, however, Pater wrote nothing beside his school themes, which, according to W. K. W. Chafy, were of a "streaming" character.

Pater, who, as we said, used to start from his home at Harbledown every morning soon after six, invariably waited for his two friends at the spot where St. Margaret's Street and Mercery Lane branch from High Street. Then the three would walk to the school round by Archdeacon Harrison's, the Dark Entry and the Deanery—the way that we represented Pater going on his first day. Near Archdeacon Harrison's was a magnificent red hawthorn, which blazed in the brilliant sunlight like a furnace of fire; and Pater, McQueen and Dombrain used to quarrel amicably about its name. Pater would call it a "red hawthorn," Dombrain a "pink hawthorn," while McQueen insisted that it was a "pink may," and no one of them ever surrendered his opinion.

29. Pater "The Saintly Boy."

In the Deanery garden was a well known mulberry tree, which used to be plentifully manured every year with bullocks' blood, which was poured into a trench round it; and Pater liked to quote an old saying: "The Dean sits under the mulberry tree till he turns purple," which had origin in the fact that many Deans of Canterbury have been advanced to the purple coat and

than cobweb, and there were thousands of names put in with painful care. The Gazetteer is alphabetical. Teabert, it seems, was a country inhabited by bad people; Dodie-land, another fanciful country, by good people or Christians, and as René himself represented the latter, he was often, at home, called Dodie, especially by his brother Robert, who, by the by, had the reputation of being a graceless Teabertian. Another volume was called "An Account of the Kingdom of Ranmark," a third "A Concise History of Jara" (capital of Dodie-land), "and of the United Empires of Jara and Tindib,[1] commonly called the Empire of Dodieland. By René el Dodie." This, in six volumes, was commenced in 1855, and went on all the time McQueen was at school with Pater. If the names of these countries, animals, &c., have Scandinavian sounds, it must be understood that to Norway, Denmark, and the Shetland Isles McQueen was always powerfully drawn. The Rainiers had been geographers and explorers pretty nearly since the time of Adam; and one of them, Peter Rainier, afterwards vice-admiral (McQueen's great-great-uncle), in company with a fellow-officer named Baker, discovered the North American mountains named after them Mount Baker and Mount Rainier—"my great-cousin" [2] as McQueen liked to call it.

One morning when René McQueen reached the Norman Staircase he saw perched on the steps, waiting for the school door to open, and peering between the little pillars at the other boys at play, a thin, plain, hump-backed, prematurely whiskered, desolate, meditative boy in cap and gown. "He had an overhanging forehead, brown hair, deep-set mild eyes near together, a nose very low at the bridge, a heavy jaw, a square chin, and a curious malformation of the mouth." Every

---

[1] City of Gold.

[2] Mt. Rainier is 14,400 feet high.

day at the same time, fearful, evidently, of being late, the same boy used to perch there among the icicles —solitary and desolate as a crane. It was Walter Pater. Odd-looking in his infancy, he had not improved with years, but if he had a plain face—an impassive frog-like face, to employ the words of one of his acquaintances— and an undignified person, his character was still of the sweetest; and his manners and his conversation—for he was fastidiously careful in his speech—had a singular charm. It was some compensation, also, to the boy to have so unusual a name, for, though only sixteen, he already had hopes of fame, and the striking name of Pater—one that had been possessed by no Englishman of distinction, seemed to him a valuable asset.

Between McQueen and Pater "a happy affinity" soon commenced; and Dombrain, already friendly with Pater, was gradually drawn into the league. The three boys (all of foreign and two of Huguenot descent) being constantly together, their schoolfellows called them "The Three Inseparables," and the Rev. George Wallace (who said they were like three cherries on a stem) "The Triumvirate"; and there is a Triumvirate, it will be remembered in *Gaston de Latour*—Jasmin, Amadée, and Camille. But though Pater took the name Triumvirate from that given to himself, McQueen and Dombrain, he does not in his book describe McQueen or Dombrain, nor is either of them the James Stokes of *Emerald Uthwart* or the Flavian of *Marius the Epicurean*; and as this narrative proceeds the reason why he did not choose to portray them will be perfectly understood. All three boys were assiduous workers, McQueen applying himself particularly to Greek and Latin, because his classical education had been much neglected before he joined the school. They were more like steady-going, hard-reading undergraduates than schoolboys, and Pater especially was not in the least like a boy, while his odd grave face and whiskered cheeks

28. The Triumvirate.

added to the appearance of manhood. Neither Pater nor McQueen ever had any desire to play or to join with the other boys in anything. Dombrain was influenced by them; and the three never played a single game with other boys all the time they were at school; and never except on one solitary occasion played a game together. This comradeship was of great help to Pater, for previously he had been merely a poor little dusty creature swept into corners, but now, with a body-guard —for he was nominally the leader—he began to assert himself—to stand up for his rights. Henceforward his life was less cramped, and his odd appearance ceased to attract ridicule; though he continued to be unpopular. All three boys were devout and good-tempered, and Mr. Wallace used to say of McQueen that he reminded him of the jolly miller who "once lived on the river Dee"— though the verse must be taken as only generally apposite; for it is not on record that any human being ever heard McQueen whistle or sing. His independence, however, was, and still is, eminently characteristic of him; and to his principles he would, and still does, adhere in spite of all appearances or consequences. We said the three strange lads never played; still they had their recreations of a kind. Their idea of a good round game was to walk together in the Precincts, and to talk about the Dean and Chapter and McQueen's Imaginary Countries, or to listen to Dombrain's tales (and the Dombrains were a family of gossips) about old Canterbury folk. Of his Imaginary Countries McQueen never tired, and he lent most of his volumes to Pater, who, however, found the kingdoms, rivers, and roads less interesting than the inhabitants who were occasionally introduced; and when he, too, took up his pen, as ultimately he did, it was also to depict imaginary persons—to present us with portraits of Marius, Gaston, Ronsard, Flavian, Brother Apollyon, Florian, Denys, Sebastian and Duke Carl. Thus Pater's bias towards portraiture of the fictitious kind exhibited itself even in "it was like a stage scene—nay! like the Middle Age itself, with this multitude of soldiers mingling in the crowd which filled the unchanged gabled streets." [1]

René McQueen—he was always called René—was a quiet, solitary, independent, and in some respects very singular boy, with strong biases and some extraordinary prejudices. Like Pater, caring nothing for games or sport, his chief amusement had been the compilation of descriptions of a number of "Imaginary Countries," some of which had been commenced at the age of six, in his father's house at Ampthill, near Bedford. A playfellow there, having once said to him boastfully, 'I'm the King of all England," little McQueen exclaimed proudly, and with a toss of the head, "I am the King of all Argent"—one of his Imaginary Countries. These descriptions were written in an exercise-book in minute writing, and illustrated with pictures of the fictitious towns, trees, animals (one was a knolvr) to be found in these lands; but later, the writing was made larger, with a view to tempting his grandmother and Walter Pater to read them. The title of one runs as follows:—

<blockquote>
The Teabertian Gazetteer
by R*** D****
Being an Accurate Description
of Every Remarkable Place
On Land or Water
In Teabert
And Dedicated By Permission
To His Majesty
King Pom
</blockquote>

3 Mar., 1853

Maps of these Imaginary Countries were also made—and wonderful maps they were—or are, for they are still preserved—done with the utmost care. The different provinces were outlined in colours as on an ordinary map, the rivers represented by wavy lines finer

---

[1] *Miscellaneous Studies*, p. 193.

purple gloves [1] that is to say to the Episcopacy. None of the three boys ever got a reproof at school, and Pater was never absent, except through illness. McQueen was late only once, and the incident had a tragic termination. The servant it seems had forgotten to call him at six. As soon as he was dressed he tore like a maniac down the hill leading from Barton Fields, but reached the Norman Staircase just too late—the last dread stroke of seven having sounded from the Cathedral clock. The door being shut, he knocked, and when Mr. Wallace re-opened it—it was to find McQueen sunk on the Staircase in a swoon, from which, however, thanks to kind words and hot coffee, he presently recovered.

As a child at Enfield, Pater had been accustomed to think of the soul as "an actual body," and of Heaven as a place with spreading cedars like those at Enfield, meandering streams, pleasant but rather artificial, like the New River, and fleshly men and women—the former tall and courtly, like Graham's "father," the latter very sweet but a little round in the back, like his darling Aunt Bessie; but his ideas had changed since then, and he would now reprove McQueen for entertaining "too material an idea of that place." McQueen, like many other boys, had a weakness for unripe fruit, and Pater one day, after solemnly enlarging upon the spiritual character of the world to come, finished up with: "One thing is quite certain, in Heaven there won't be any heavenly green apples."

Pater and McQueen were very often at Dombrain's house in St. Margaret's Street, where the fun was generally charades, at which Pater excelled, and where they continued to meet the Rev. E. H. Woodall, whose influence, as the following incident shows, had by this time made itself strongly felt. One morning as Pater and McQueen were passing between Canon Moore's house and Archdeacon Harrison's, the conversation happening to turn upon the merits and demerits of

---

[1] Formerly worn by bishops.

Protestantism and Catholicism, Pater observed: "Protestantism is the only religion without a sacrifice" —an idea which he certainly may have taken from a book by Robert Wilberforce,[1] who went over to Rome, but which he probably obtained from Mr. Woodall.

"That," followed McQueen, "is not true, as we accept, and trust to, the *one* oblation and sacrifice of Himself made by Christ on the cross—made once and for ever."

In his pleasing "In Memoriam, W.H.P."[2] the Rev. Dr. Bussell, a friend of Pater's last few years, notices that "child-like simplicity, that naïve joyousness, that never-wearying pleasure in animals and their ways, that grave yet half-amused seriousness, also childlike, in which Pater met the events of the daily routine"; and Mr. McQueen, commenting on the passage, observes: "This, together with his piety, was what particularly charmed me in the Pater of 1855 and later." In after years, describing the Pater of this period, Mr. McQueen referred to him as "The saintly boy."

[1] Brother of the Bishop.
[2] A sermon preached 14th October 1894.

CHAPTER IX

THE REV. GEORGE WALLACE AGAIN

30. Rev. George Wallace again.

That Pater was never a popular boy at King's School is not surprising, seeing that he avoided almost every one except Dombrain and McQueen. Nor did the Rev. George Wallace really take to him, while Pater, on his part, was never attracted to Mr. Wallace. "You, McQueen and Dombrain are a great deal too much together," he would say to Pater, "you are like the Twelve Apostles [1] at Cambridge, and I am sure you would have far more influence for good in the school if only you would mingle with the other boys." But the three not only took no notice of his words, they became more engrossed in each other every day, and what one did all did. If, however, Pater rather disliked Mr. Wallace, he always respected him for his wide learning and especially for his knowledge of history, literature, and theology. Loving English literature for its own sake, he often used to read to the boys passages from Shakespeare, *Paradise Lost* and *The Task,* and he familiarised them not only with Homer but also with Cowper's translation. Variable in his moods, being at one time much on the alert, and at others rather dreamy, he, nevertheless, could always appreciate a joke, and when in the mood to be pleasant with the class would make atrocious puns; and the audible groans with which they were received never failed to put him into still better humour. Among the boys in the Fifth Form to which Pater had by this time risen was a Pope and also an Abbot; and Mr. Wallace,

---

[1] Tennyson, Hallam, and ten others, 1828—1831.

who called them his "three fathers," used to observe that it was a singular circumstance that in a form consisting of only a dozen boys three should be called "father" in different languages.[1]

Whatever his troubles at school, Pater had at least one distinct consolation. Notwithstanding his simious, hairy face, and prodigious chin, there was one of his schoolfellows who was even plainer—a boy named Jones. It was said that Pater and Jones seemed to be having a perpetual contest to see which could look the uglier; but Jones, by universal consent, bore away the apple. When Jones's appearance was commented upon, Pater listened with complaisance, and at other times he himself made many a quietly sardonic remark on the subject; for Pater, though his books do not reveal it, had, life through, an abundance of wit. A good deal of the boys' time was spent in the old schoolroom, which had a long table down the middle shaped like the letter T, and the three Inseparables used to sit outside the cross-piece, and facing the length of the table, that is at the end farthest from Mr. Wallace's house. One day after lessons, while they were chatting together, a number of other boys, among whom was Jones, began quarrelling. All of a sudden there was a scuffle. Forms fell, boys shouted, books flew, fists rose. Jones and another boy grappled each other, and the hubbub was perfect. Suddenly Jones was flung on to the floor, and while the ungainly lad was floundering about, Pater, snatching up a large key (probably that of his locker), and holding the handle to his eye, said, with a ridiculous drawl, and while bending on him a scrutinizing glance: "Is that a fair young girl?"—putting a strong emphasis on the last word. The comical action, the remark, and the knowledge that Pater was none too beautiful himself, raised a roar of laughter, and chiefly at the expense of

31. Pater's Rival.

[1] Pater (Latin), Pope (Middle English), Abbot (Syriac). See Romans VIII., 15).

L

poor Jones, but it also had the effect of restoring good feeling, and the quarrel was forgotten.

No one can think of Walter Pater's school days without recalling that charming piece of tesselated work *Emerald Uthwart*. Emerald Uthwart is,

32. Emerald Uthwart. as we said, an ideal Pater—what Pater would have been glad to look back upon as himself. Of the probable origin of the surname we have already spoken.[1] Chase Lodge, Emerald's birthplace, took its name from Chase Side, Pater's home at Enfield, but Emerald's village is apparently Chailey in Sussex, of which we shall speak later. The resemblances between Emerald and Pater are principally in their characters—for, if Pater intended Emerald for himself exteriorly, his memory must have been sadly at fault. Emerald at the King's School, Canterbury, was a "Young Apollo"—"Golden-haired, scholar Apollo" passers-by repeated "foolishly, ignorantly," and very ignorant and foolish a passer-by would have been to make that remark of Pater. Then again, Emerald was a capital cricketer. Did he not once make a wonderful hit—sending a ball right over the lime-trees and the Cathedral roof and onward into space till at last in despair of ever coming down it stayed where it was and turned into a star! Alas! Pater knew nothing of cricket—scarcely knew which was the right side of the bat. A ball delivered to him would be more likely, instead of rising above the cathedral, to knock over his wickets, unless he had himself already knocked them over in his clumsy endeavours to hit it. Emerald Uthwart went soldiering.[2] Pater, in a scarlet jacket with black facings, would have been a sight for gods and men. But, life through, Pater the weakling was all admiration for the strong,[3] Pater the unathletic for the agile, Pater the timid for the bold and aggressive,

[1] Chapter I.
[2] Here perhaps Pater was thinking of his brother William, who always had a hankering after a soldier's life.
[3] See Chapter XXXI.

Pater the plain for the æsthetic and beautiful, and especially for the creature of "immature radiance"[1]—nay, he was himself to become the very hierophant of culture.

There is no reference to football in *Emerald Uthwart*, but it was a popular game at the King's School. Instead of goal-posts the boys marked on two opposite walls of the Green Court two upright lines, of which those on the west wall may still be seen, with the letters "L.G." (lower goal) painted between them.

If in some respects Pater and Emerald differed widely, they resembled each other largely in character. The descriptions, too, of the King's School and the Precincts are minutely accurate. We recognise the scholars in their gowns and caps (though he calls the monitors "prefects"), the rambling houses of the prebends, the architectural glories of the Cathedral, the Dark Entry, the old schoolroom and the ways and customs of the school. He notes, too, the scaffold poles always to be found somewhere about the Cathedral—a reference, no doubt, to the restoration of Trinity Chapel and the erection of the figures of the Evangelists near Becket's Crown—but he always preferred to see scaffold poles about a magnificent pile.[2] If in *Emerald Uthwart* there are memories of Pater's schooldays, there are memories, too, in *Marius* and *Gaston de Latour*. Young Marius with his religious predilections and joy in priestly ceremonies is, in a manner, Pater's own self; and we remember how lovingly Pater dwells on the "traditional Christian pieties of the Chateau of Deux-Manoirs."

It is characteristic of Pater that the part of the Cathedral by which he was most attracted was the "Warriors' Chapel," for though he was never at any part of his life, or in any sense, a fighting man, nevertheless, as "Emerald Uthwart" would alone prove, he was

33. The Warriors' Chapel.

---

[1] Greek Stud., p. 185.
[2] See Chapter XXII.

curiously attracted by war and warriors—battle and murder and sudden death. These, of course, were bustling times. It was the second year of the Crimean War. Inkermann had been fought 5th November, 1854. On 8th September, 1855, Sebastopol was evacuated. From time immemorial there had been a military garrison at Canterbury, and sons of officers in the school. McQueen, his great friend, as we have seen, was the son of an officer, and "uniforms and surplices were always close together" at service in the choir—especially on Sunday afternoons. "A military tradition had been continuous from the days of crusading knights who lay humbly on their backs in the 'Warriors' Chapel' to the time of the Civil Wars, when a certain heroic youth of eighteen was brought to rest there, and so on to the present time." [1] Every object in this chapel was stereotyped in Pater's mind—the alabaster tomb in the centre, representing Lady Margaret Holland and her two husbands, John Earl of Somerset [2] and the Duke of Clarence (son of Henry IV.); [3] the tomb of Stephen Langton, projecting from the east wall; the bust of Admiral Rooke; and the monument to Thomas Thornhurst [4] of the unfortunate Isle of Rhé expedition.

Among his schoolfellows was a well-built, supple, handsome, aristocratic-looking, violent lad named Joseph Haydock, whose father, a retired officer, resided in Chantry Lane off the New Dover Road; and Pater, who had a passion for everything handsome and beautiful, regarded Haydock almost with adoration. The youthful Apollo—and he really was an Apollo—never, however, reciprocated this feeling, or ever troubled himself about Pater at all; which was for Pater's good, for, beyond physical beauty, Haydock

34. Joseph Haydock.

[1] "Emerald Uthwart," *Mis. Stud.*, p. 193.
[2] He died 1409.
[3] Killed at Beaugy in France 1421.
[4] 1627.

seems not to have had a great deal in him that was enviable. Haydock, who may be the Exmes in *Gaston de Latour*—"tall Exmes, lithe and cruel like a tiger—whom it was pleasant to stroke"—was not liked in the school, nor, considering his hectoring ways, is it surprising, and he gloried in the fact. Pater and McQueen used to compare their schoolfellows to various animals, and there is an echo of this amusement in *Gaston de Latour,* where it is observed: "The tiger was there, the parrot, the hare, the goat of course, and certainly much apishness"[1] Other boys were compounds: the griffin, the wyvern, and other fearsome beasts that W. K. W. Chafy was supposed to ride, and, no doubt, did ride—in his dreams. "And what am I like?" demanded Haydock. "A handsome, ferocious young bull," replied Pater, and Haydock seemed pleased.

Our chief interest in Haydock is on account of the fact that as to externals—and it may be noted that on leaving school he entered the army—he is supposed to be the James Stokes of *Emerald Uthwart*. In character, love for study and quickness of perception, James Stokes has resemblances to McQueen. But the ground is not covered even by these statements. Thus Stokes was a "very Kentish lad," whereas Haydock was of Lancashire stock,[2] and McQueen was Celtic—for of his four grandparents not one was of English descent. The latter part of *Emerald Uthwart* is pure imagination.

The School Speech day, with its usual ceremonies, had now come round again, but while McQueen received prizes for French and Classics, and both he and Dombrain were otherwise commended, Pater obtained no distinction.

35. The School Speech Day, Sept., 1855.

[1] Gaston, p. 43.
[2] There is a Father Haydocke in Ainsworth's *Lancashire Witches*. Ainsworth knew the history of Lancashire thoroughly.

CHAPTER X

JANUARY 1856 TO MAY 1856

S. ELIZABETH AND OTHER POEMS

BIBLIOGRAPHY :

1. St. Elizabeth of Hungary, Spring 1856.
2. The Chant of the Celestial Sailors, Spring 1856.
3. Poets Old and New, August 1856.

Two events mark the opening of 1856—the first being Pater's confirmation—the Triumvirate (for they were even confirmed together) having presented themselves on 26th March before Archbishop Sumner;[1] the other the blossoming of Pater as a poet. It has been ignorantly alleged by previous writers (and one has followed another like Carlyle's sheep jumping over an imaginary stick) that although Pater's earliest published essays are as mature in style as the author was mature in years, Pater made no attempt to write either as a schoolboy or as an undergraduate. But this is a colossal mistake, for not only was Pater one of the most prolific schoolboy authors who ever lived; but as an undergraduate, he wrote something or other—a poem, a translation, a portion of an essay—almost every day, while at the King's School he composed, in addition to the "streaming themes" laid before good Mr. Fisher, scores of poems, many elaborate essays, and a number of long stories. It was his custom to enter the poems in a manuscript book kept for the purpose, and then to make copies for those of his friends who begged them. The best seem to have appeared in print—having possibly been contributed to the Poet's

36. Saint Elizabeth of Hungary.

---

[1] John Bird Sumner became Archbishop of Canterbury in 1848. He died 6th September 1862.

Corner of some country newspaper.⁽¹⁾ Between 1856 and 1860 he wrote scores of poems, and a number of them, in his own handwriting and signed, are in the possession of his friends. The story of the destruction of the manuscript book will be told by and by.⁽²⁾

The earliest of his poems in our possession is entitled "St. Elizabeth of Hungary," and bears date January, 1856, but he had written many others previously. The subject was avowedly suggested by the perusal of Kingsley's dramatic poem, *The Saint's Tragedy, or the True Story of Saint Elizabeth of Hungary,* which appeared in 1848,⁽³⁾ and excited wide-spread interest—among its admirers being the Prince Consort. Kingsley's poem (need one say?) was written in opposition to asceticism; and in his preface the author girds at "those miserable *dilettanti,* who, in books and sermons, are whimpering meagre second-hand phrases of celibacy, deprecating as carnal and degrading those family ties, to which they owe their own existence." But Pater, whose heroes were St. Paul and Hippolytus, whose heroines St. Apollonia and Diana, takes the opposite view—and cannot sufficiently praise the beauty and holiness of celibacy.

St. Elizabeth, the subject of his poem, was born in Hungary of royal parentage in 1207, and at the age of 14 married Louis IV. Landgraf of Thuringia, who held his court in the Wartburg, near Eisenach. Her piety, self-denial and almsgiving occasioned wide-spread comment; and her life was a happy one until 1227, when, her husband having been killed in the Crusades, her brother-in-law drove her from the country. Assisted by her friends she regained her position; and this accomplished, she put on nun's raiment, renounced

---

⁽¹⁾ Pater told his friends that some of his early writings had been printed.

⁽²⁾ Chapter XXIV.

⁽³⁾ The Second Edition (1851) has a Preface by Professor Maurice.

the world, devoted her revenues to the poor, and took up her residence with her three children in a cottage near her castle of Marburg, which she occupied till her death, in 1231, at the early age of 24. Pater's poem, in which her story—a favourite one with painters and poets, is handled with freedom, commences:

> In Wartburgh's stately pile she dwelt, as years went slowly by;

and the saint is represented as fixing her thoughts on Heaven and as living, although married, in a state of virginity.

> Within her lamp there brightly burned a pure ethereal flame,
> And so she waited till the great Celestial Bridegroom came.

Pater's enthusiasm for celibacy led him to ignore the fact that Elizabeth had three children, but then to adhere to historical facts when dealing with the life of a saint would have been contrary to all precedents, and it is not for us to frown at Pater for not deviating from a fine old crusted rule; besides, the assumption that she remained a virgin, though married, gives point to the stanza just quoted about the "pure ethereal flame," and makes possible its agreeable concluding line. The second and third stanzas describe her works of charity and the difficulties she encountered. She is then represented as coming down the steep castle hill on a wintry day carrying in her vest some food provided for the poor. But she is overtaken by her husband, with whose "stern command" she is bound to comply. He enquires why she is abroad, says that such acts are far beneath his "castle's stately dame," and shakes rudely her laden vest. Wonderful to say, there falls upon the snowy ground, not the food she has carried, but a shower of blossoms, which, with their rich perfume, load the ambient air. Here again history is flouted, for Elizabeth's husband, who thoroughly sympathised with her, would have been the last man to object to her charity. However, according to tradition, the miracle really took place, though the name of the offender is not transmitted; but it does not in the least matter, and Pater's moral is unexceptionable. The flowers of "sunny climes," he says, may be bright and odorous, but far brighter and sweeter are the flowers that bloom on "Faith's eternal tree." Every deed of love we do will prove an amaranthine blossom, and, when the toils of life are over, the reward will be "a cross of light—Christ's own eternal peace."

The next poem, "The Chant of the Celestial Sailors," which is simply a jingle of musical words, is supposed to be sung by the Christian pilgrim as he journeys to Heaven, not, however, by that boggy, thorny, uncomfortable road, beset with scowling giants and gaping hobgoblins, that John Bunyan made, but sybaritically by boat over a violet sea—with neither hurricane nor sea-snake to hinder.

> Every wave behind us glancing
> Wears a crest of snow-white foam,
> Like the matin cloud advancing,
> In the blue ethereal dome.

They proceed to Heaven so pleasantly that they have no need even to row. Angels speed them

> o'er the surging
> Bosom of the billowy sea,

which would have just suited Pater, with his very elementary knowledge of boating. Starting at sunset, they proceed all night, wafted by those angels' wings, and early next morning their song mingles with the "angels' song celestial." The superiority of Pater's route to Bunyan's will at once be conceded when we point out that the voyage, besides being delightful, was all over in eight hours; whereas Bunyan's route—to say nothing of the bundle—used to occupy years.

Of a poem that Pater wrote subsequently, "The Chant of the Celestial Sailors when they first put out to Sea," we shall speak in a later chapter. Pater took more delight in the ancient English poets than in the moderns, and he warmly praises the former at the expense of the latter in his verses entitled "Poets Old and New," which are dated August, 1856. In former days, he says, the poet lived " 'mid mountains wild," or in "green and golden-vested woods"—sitting in their "sunny glades" from daybreak to sunset and weaving their golden songs in silence. But now the poet haunts the roaring street and forsakes the moon for the lamp. The poet in old times used to sing of labour and war, but the modern minstrel can find praise only for "peace." They no longer, cries the bellicose Pater, bid men fight for others and lift their hearts to Heaven.

> The poet tells no more of champions brave,
> In war's dark close oppressed;
> But with a lowlier tone, in accents grave,
> He sings—Rest! Rest!

Although Pater criticised the moderns so severely there was one of their number whom he always excepted, namely, Wordsworth, a large copy of whose poems was among his dearest treasures.[1] He longed to have his name coupled with that of Wordsworth and to see "S. Elizabeth and other Poems" exposed for sale in shop windows by the side of "The Excursion";—indeed the fame that Marius conceived for himself in his boyhood was of the "intellectual order, that of a poet perhaps." Mention Wordsworth, indeed, and Pater's eyes, usually so calm and meek, burnt instantly with a strange fire; and years after, when he wished to pay Mrs. Humphry Ward a special compliment he said "She is a true disciple in the school of Wordsworth."

He, too, would become a great poet, and write verses sufficiently sweet to make the heavenly gods

> break off their nectar draughts,
> And lay their ears down to the lowly earth.

But Fate, we need hardly say, had marked out for him an altogether different career from that which he

---

[1] See Chapter XVIII.

had just then been imagining. However, for the present he went on composing his poems—copies of which he presented to Dombrain and McQueen; and later some of them drifted to his cousin Mira,[1] daughter of his uncle William. Mira, who, as we have seen, had been left an orphan at the early age of three, had never since met her cousins. Their Aunt Bessie, however, who had long been anxious that the young people should know one another, especially as the families had been estranged, made it her business to bring them together—a kind action that gave the good soul satisfaction all her life. To Mira, who was just seventeen, Pater became sincerely attached—though his attachment to any one—whether of the fair sex or his own—never went beyond a very moderate degree of temperature. From both men and women he always attracted more love than he returned, and two of Pater's friends have observed to the writer—using almost identically the same words—"I am sure he did not feel for me the affection I felt for him." In addition to presenting Mira with his poems, he wrote for her a long story, which, unfortunately, is lost.

[1] Now Mrs. Goodwin.

CHAPTER XI

MAY 1856

THE BLEAN WOODS

The favourite haunts of the Triumvirate were what Pater called "the green and golden-vested Blean Woods"—the remains of an ancient forest between Faversham and Canterbury, including Bigberry Wood, with its old British camp, a little to the south of Harbledown, Howth Wood, "the wildest place near Canterbury," and Bosenden Wood, associated with a religious enthusiast named Thom, *alias* "Sir William Percy Honywood Courtenay, Knight of Malta and King of Jerusalem." A man of magnificent physique with handsome features and a raven-black beard, Thom generally appeared in a resplendent tunic, upon the breast of which was embroidered a golden Maltese Cross; a cloak of Tyrian purple; a Spanish sombrero; and with a long sword, which he called Excalibur, at his thigh.

37. The Blean Woods, May, 1856.

> My flowing robe, my flowing beard, my horse with flowing mane, sirs;
> They stared—the days of chivalry, they thought, were come again, sirs! [1]

Finally Thom gave out that he was the Messiah. He promptly shot dead Lieutenant Bennet, who had been sent with a party to arrest him; but was himself killed shortly after at a spot in the wood now called Mad Thom's Corner.

Dombrain, who was deeply impressed by the sinister

---

[1] Ainsworth's *Rookwood*, Ch. XXI. This song, "The Knight of Malta," accurately describes the earlier career of Thom in Kent.

story—who, indeed, revelled in everything legendary or historical relating to Canterbury—told Pater that the common people, who were dazzled by Courtenay's chivalric pomp, and had been extraordinarily devoted to him, always said that he had either not died or would come to life again.

The three boys used to call their pastimes in the woods "skirmishing"—a word settled by Pater, with his military instincts. "Skirmishing" was always pleasant, but never so delightful as in spring, when the hawthorn hedges and the oak-shaws were burgeoning. There were anemones in every thicket and hyacinths reaching to the knee. The hyacinth, with its graceful dark blue bells was one of Pater's favourite flowers, despite its "heavy and narcotic aroma,"[1] a characteristic, however, which, he declared, had been common to all spring flowers since the days of Proserpine; while the yellow archangel recommended itself if only by its ecclesiastical name. When the three strange boys were tired of romping about, or of making a dam—"'our breakwater'"[2] as they called it—in one of the tiny streams, Dombrain would tell once more the lurid story of Mad Thom of the coal-black beard; or another favourite yarn of his— that of the audacious Canterbury goldsmith, at the time of the passing of the Reform Bill, who hooted and stoned Archbishop Howley.[3] McQueen would speak of new features which he meant to insert in his "Imaginary Countries"; and Pater would recall Chaucer's pilgrims or tell tales of holy virgin and saint with macerated faces and hollow eyes as if cut out of old yellow ivory, of priest in flowered amice and stole, or of gorgeous but noseless and fingerless abbots kneeling in dim earthy churches with their palms pressed in prayer.

Another resort of the Triumvirate was Blaxlands, a

[1] *Greek Studies*, p. 116.
[2] See Chapter XXIII., p. 81.
[3] Howley crowned Queen Victoria. He died in 1848, and was succeeded by Sumner.

picturesque and idyllic tree-cinctured farm, belonging to Dombrain's father, situated four miles to the north-east of Canterbury and near their beloved Blean Woods. They had many junketings there, especially when the cherries were ripe—and while they ate the good fruit their eyes often rested on the abundant supply of evil fruit—the hawks, stoats, starlings and weasels—that hung head-downwards from the branches. But the greatest treat of all was when the good folks at the farm brought "syllabubs under the cow"—namely, spice, wine and sugar "and the cow milked into it." [1] A short cut or bridle-way led through the woods to the north-east and came out on an upland above Herne village, a few miles from Herne Bay, and in the middle of that wood was a fir plantation and an amphitheatre of wood with a good echo. "On one occasion," says J. R. McQueen, "we played here a game of trap ball—the only time that I remember Pater playing a regular game."

The road through the village of Harbledown was part of the old Pilgrim's Way to the Shrine of S. Thomas a Beckett; and in the middle of the village stands the Hospital of S. Nicholas, at which the pilgrims used to make offerings. Both the hospital and its church still attract large numbers of visitors. An ancient verger, in whom the history of the place has rooted itself as the ivy in the tower, points out each hoary characteristic of the church: the frescoes which dimly cover the walls, the old benches made so that the worshippers sat back to back—surely the most aged wooden seats in the world, the extraordinary floor, sloping from the chancel to the west door, the Norman arches, the ancient glass, showing that well known garden flower, the Canterbury bell. He then conducts the visitor to the Hospital and shows its treasures—cups, mazers or drinking bowls, in

38. The Hospital of S. Nicholas.

---

[1] Recollections of these joys are possibly interwoven in his sketch of Watteau, *Imag. Port.*, p. 13.

one of which glitters the crystal that "embellished the buckle of S. Thomas's shoe," a pilgrim's pouch, an antique incense pot, and a primitive money-box. The last and the crystal are the objects referred to by Erasmus, who, speaking of a journey made with Colet through the village, says : "On the left side of the road is an almshouse of some old men, one of whom runs out as soon as they perceive a horseman approaching, and after sprinkling him with holy water, offers him the upper leather of a shoe bound with brass, in which a piece of glass is set like a gem. This is kissed, and money given him." When Colet was asked to kiss the crystal he became offensive. So Erasmus "took compassion on the old man and gave him money by way of consolation." These various treasures are now secure behind plate-glass, but it was Pater's boast that on one occasion when visiting the Hospital he touched the crystal. The Black Prince's well, with its keystone carved into ostrich feathers, at the back of the Hospital, was also a favourite resort of the Triumvirate, who wrangled amicably, as so many have wrangled amicably before and since, concerning its supposed medical properties, and the probability of the truth of the tradition that its water was drunk by the Black Prince on his sick bed. With the chaplain of the Hospital, the Rev. Charles William Bewsher, Vicar of Nackington, who, as a set-off against a small income, had an enormous family, the Paters were on terms of intimacy, and Pater and Mr. Bewsher's son, Charles Edward, were bosom friends previous to the formation of the Triumvirate.

Another of Pater's resorts was Bishopsbourne, associated with his great idol, Richard Hooker, who there (1595-1600) finished his famous *Ecclesiastical Polity*. In the words of Izaak Walton : "This parsonage of Bourne is from Canterbury three miles, and near to the common road that leads from that city to Dover; in which

39. Bishopsbourne.

parsonage Mr. Hooker had not been twelve months, but his books and the innocency and sanctity of his life became so remarkable, that many turned out of the road, and others—scholars especially—went purposely to see the man whose life and learning were so much admired"; and many others, we may add, have since his death, found their way to the church to see his effigy in cap and gown, and the inscription (by Sir William Cowper) in which he is called "Judicious Hooker." *The Ecclesiastical Polity* was one of Pater's greatest enthusiasms, and he knew by heart the whole of Keble's abbreviation [1] of the Fifth Book.

On the 29th of May, 1856, there were rejoicings all over the country on account of the conclusion of peace with Russia. The Canterbury church towers and inn doors burst suddenly into green, the city banner, with its three Cornish choughs, blew out stiffly, and every house displayed the Union Jack or the Kentish horse; while the King's School boys, with sprigs of oak in their buttonholes, processioned to the special service in the Cathedral, where they offered thanks to "Almighty God"—"for that signal and wonderful deliverance vouchsafed to their then most gracious Sovereign King Charles the Second, and all the Royal Family, and in them to this whole Church and State, and all orders and degrees of men in both, from the unnatural Rebellion, Usurpation, and Tyranny of ungodly and cruel men, and from the sad confusions and ruin thereupon ensuing," [2] and having suitably honoured the memory of the saintly Sovereign they were given the rest of the day as a holiday, most of which they spent in piously pinching the arms and thighs of sinful boys who had neglected to show their oak.

40. The Peace Rejoicings, 29th May, 1856.

[1] This, says Mr. McQueen, was one of the books in which we were examined, I think, in 1857. The compilation made a small neat book.

[2] See Prayer Books previous to 1857, "Restoration of the Royal Family."

THE BLEAN WOODS

Owing to the teaching of the ritualistic Rev. E. H. Woodall, Dombrain had always been very "High," and Pater had by this time become almost as pronounced in his opinions; but McQueen, who was uninfluenced by Mr. Woodall, returned later to Evangelicalism, of which he is to-day one of the stoutest supporters in his county. The three boys not only attended cheerfully the usual school services at the Cathedral, but also, of their own accord, many other services—a proceeding that occasioned among their schoolfellows, who preferred cricket to collect, unqualified amazement.

41. High Church.

When home for his holidays, Pater, who (in the words of a cousin), was "a tremendous Ritualist," would never eat meat in Lent, and his deportment towards those who did was cold and constrained. The Breviary was as much his companion as the Prayer Book, and every night he said the prayer for peace: *"Deus, a quo sancta desideria, recta consilia et justa sunt opera; da servis tuis illam, quam mundus dare non potest, pacem; ut et corda nostra mandatis tuis dedita et hostium sublata formidine, tempora sint tua protectione tranquilla. Per Dominum nostrum Jesum Christum. Amen."*

The story of the Triumvirate, indeed—of those odd boys who spent their pocket money on books of devotion, and stole away from school games to attend service at church—reads not unlike a page from some mediæval Lives of the Saints.

CHAPTER XII

JULY 1856 TO DECEMBER 1856.

A SERIOUS ILLNESS.

42. Pater injured in a scuffle. (probably Aug. 1856.)

In the autumn of this year there occurred to Pater a serious misfortune. As we have seen, he had never been popular at school, and one day, for a reason not known—perhaps for no particular reason—a number of the boys set upon him near the Norman Staircase; and in the midst of the scuffle a ruffianly boy, whose name may be omitted, gave Pater a dreadful kick, with the result that he had at once to be conveyed home, where he lay ill for many weeks. Mr. Wallace, having been informed of the name of the offender, not only took the matter up, but expressed his determination to expel him from the school. From Pater, however, on his sick bed came an earnest request that the boy might be forgiven, and the affair passed over. This magnanimity affected Mr. Wallace even to tears, and as late as two years after, when bidding Pater farewell, he told him that he had not forgotten "that beautiful act of Christian Charity;" [1] while Pater's magnanimity became one of the prized traditions of the school. From the results of this lamentable occurrence, however, he never, it has been assumed, really recovered, and the peculiarity of his gait which marked him all the rest of his life is attributable to it.

[1] See Chapter XVII.

A SERIOUS ILLNESS

In the meantime Speech Day had come round again, and Pater, McQueen and Dombrain, all in Form 5, obtained rewards for Classics. As Pater lay ill at Harbledown, Dombrain received the prize for him; and Mr. Wallace, when handing the book, made the observation: "I am sorry for his absence, still more sorry for the cause."

43. The School Speech Day, Sept., 1856, Mr. Sankey leaves.

McQueen won the Tenterden Prize for History, and he and Dombrain obtained various other "rewards."[1]

Another event of this Speech Day was the farewell made by the Rev. Philip Menzies Sankey, who had been presented to the curacy of Highclere in Hampshire—an event which, as we shall presently see, was to have a very romantic sequel.[2]

---

[1] Among the "speeches" were—
   Dombrain, Satan, Par. Lost IV.
   Robert McQueen, Cowper's Task, Bk. VI., 759.
Not only is Pater's name absent from the list of speech-makers, Rainier McQueen's name is absent too.

[2] See Chapter XXI.

CHAPTER XIII

JANUARY AND FEBRUARY 1857

DEATH OF DEAN LYALL

44. The Death of Dean Lyall, Feb., 1857.
In February, 1857, occurred the long-expected death of the invalided Dean Lyall, and the hope was expressed that Lord Palmerston, who was then Premier, would allow the body to be buried within the Precincts. But the reply being a refusal, accompanied by a brutal comment, it was decided that the interment should take place at Harbledown. The funeral was one of the most imposing ever witnessed in Canterbury, and crowds filled the Cathedral and the streets.

As regards the school, it was decided that only the King's Scholars should take part in the proceedings. Consequently, while Pater and Dombrain were entitled to go, McQueen was excluded.

"I am very sorry," observed McQueen, "for I particularly wanted to attend."

"Take my place, then," said Dombrain, "I will lend you my gown." So, the Rev. George Wallace, consenting, McQueen put on the gown, though, before he had worn it many minutes, he had the misfortune to tear it badly. The procession started from the King's School. First went the Beadsmen, with badges on their cloaks, then the Rev. Anby Beatson and the King's Scholars, including Pater and McQueen, in Dombrain's torn gown, the Rev. George Wallace, the Precentor, the Minor Canons, the "Six Preachers," and other Cathedral dignitaries. Lastly came the body and the mourners. Pater was profoundly impressed both by the service—held in the nave of the Cathedral, which was draped with black and crowded to the very doors—

and by the singing of the final hymn: "The righteous souls that wing their flight"; and scarcely less impressed by the crowds in the streets and at the windows and balconies as the procession moved to Harbledown.

The Triumvirate, who had always listened with rapt attention to the sermons of Vice-Dean Harrison, whom they truly loved and reverenced, had hoped that he would be Dean Lyall's successor; but, to their intense disappointment, the cloak fell on the plentifully-bearded, shaven-lipped, shambling Henry Alford — who is now chiefly remembered as the writer of "A Plea for the Queen's English" and the popular hymn commencing "Come, ye thankful people, come." Dean Alford, who had been appointed on March 6th, was "read in" on April 19th; and in a letter to a friend,[1] he tells how he was led into the Cathedral by the canons, how Canon Harrison, a ripe, though somewhat stiff scholar . . . . a friendly Christian fellow . . . . recited a Latin collect when placing him in the stall, how he was taken to the Prior's stone seat in the Chapter House and there swore "a monstrous long oath without," he believed, "any false quantities," and how the canons, one and all, came and vowed obedience to him.

45. Dean Alford.

Excellent man though he was, Alford had neither tact nor, as the following incident will illustrate, the slightest sympathy for the *genius loci* of Canterbury. A stained-glass window, the prevailing tints of which were green and yellow, having been placed in the Warriors' Chapel to the memory of the Buffs who fell in the Crimean War, Alford went with a select company to inspect it. While he attentively gazed at it, everyone waited with expectancy for some glowing remark—some burst of poetry—something to treasure through life—and at last it came. Turning from the window to the company, he observed gravely: "Sage and onions."

[1] Rev. C. Merivale. See Life of Dean Alford by his widow 1873. Alford died 12th January 1871.

Alluding to Alford's very awkward gait, Pater remarked that he walked as if he expected to be kicked; and he declared that the very thought of Alford's long and dreary sermons, delivered with a decided Somerset accent, made him melancholy as a gib cat. Perhaps, however, Pater was scarcely just to the new dean, and we like to think that the painstaking scholar who just then and later lectured so much and talked so earnestly about the Queen's English had a little—just a very little—to do with the formation of Pater's style. However, appreciate the Dean or not, the Triumvirate were obliged to have him, and often; for whereas Lyall had been accustomed to occupy the pulpit only three times a year, Alford took upon himself when in residence to preach every afternoon.

The Triumvirate did not forget each other's birthdays, but the presents given and accepted were such as they and they alone would ever have thought of. Thus on 3rd March, 1857, McQueen's birthday, Pater handed his friend a copy of Bishop Andrewes' *Manual of Devotion*[1]—a favourite with himself—though he was equally attached to Williams's *Cathedral*[2] and the religious poems of Henry Vaughan.[3] Another present received by McQueen that year was "a perspective pocket glass," sent him by his mother, who was staying at Cheltenham. In her letter which accompanied it she said, "One does see very clear with it, but you must not expect to distinguish Pater at Harbledown when you are standing on the Dane John Mount[4] or anything like it."

---

[1] Lancelot Andrewes, successively Bishop of Chichester, Ely, and Winchester [1555—1626]. His *Manual of Devotion* in Greek and Latin was translated by George Stanhope, Dean of Canterbury (1714—1766).

[2] Rev. Isaac Williams (1802—1865), Tractarian Friend of Keble.

[3] Henry Vaughan (1614—1695). In *Plato and Platonism*, "The Doctrine of Number," Pater quotes almost the whole of Vaughan's poem, "The Retreat."

[4] A high mound in Canterbury.

M. MARTINET,

FRENCH MASTER AT THE KING'S SCHOOL.

REV. JOHN BACHELOR KEARNEY.

TAKEN IN 1869.

About this time a Special Department was formed in the School—for backward and unruly boys—and also for boys who were to enter the army instead of proceeding to a University. Of the master appointed, the Rev. John Bachelor Kearney, it was said, in reference to the turbulence of his pupils, "He fought, and not unsuccessfully, with beasts at Ephesus." Mr. Kearney was a tall rather gaunt reddish-haired man, with a good, honest, rugged face—a face so like that of Holman Hunt's "Light of the World," that Mr. Kearney might have been the model. He had a slightly abrupt, uncouth manner, and was endowed with much *bonhomie,* a valuable possession to one so peculiarly situated, and both McQueen and Pater, who often met him at Dombrain's house, derived continual amusement from his whimsical sallies. At the same time they thoroughly respected him, particularly on account of his attainments as a scholar, and he on his part had a sincere regard not only for their personal but also for their spiritual welfare—a feeling, however, which, as we shall see, had presently the result of erecting between him and Pater an impenetrable barrier. Pater was also very frequently at McQueen's house, No. 3, Barton Fields, where he met McQueen's grandmother, Mrs. Rainier, "a queenly woman," who took a great liking to him, and who often, by her cheering and stimulating words, encouraged him in his efforts at school.[1]

46. Rev. John Bachelor Kearney, Oct., 1856.

[1] See also Chapter XVII.

CHAPTER XIV

MARCH 1857—JULY 1857

CASSANDRA

BIOGRAPHY :
4. Cassandra (poem), 1857, June 29th.

47.
Cassandra,
June, 1857.

One sunny June morning, while Pater and McQueen were sitting under an oak in the Precincts, Pater drew from his pocket a newly-written, mournful and slightly sensual poem called "Cassandra"; and then, in compliance with his friend's request, read it aloud. It was the story of the unfortunate prophetess of Antiquity. According to Æschylus,[1] Cassandra, when in the height of her loveliness, made a request to Apollo, whose priestess she was, for the augmentation of her prophetic powers—a request which he readily granted upon her promising to respond to his love. No sooner, however, had she obtained the gift than she refused point blank to fulfil her portion of the covenant;[2] whereupon the offended Apollo, unwilling or unable to revoke the gift, informed her that, although she would have abnormal prophetic powers, her predictions would never be believed. Calamity followed calamity, and Pater's poem opens with a lament supposed to have been uttered by Cassandra on one of the brass-beaked galleys after her capture by the Greeks. She compares herself to a stricken hart around

[1] Agamemnon.

[2] Cf. Æschylus, "First I assented, then deceived the God" (Agamemnon).

whom his captors stand jesting; and, in the hope of obtaining help and comfort, she apostrophises the ocean, the queen of Heaven and great Agamemnon; but all are deaf or indifferent—and she bursts out into a wild cry of lamentation.

Then turning to Apollo, whom she reminds of that happy morning in spring when he knelt at her side, she implores him in agonized words to revoke his terrible gift, assures him that in those days she loved him with a passion never lavished on mortals, and continues:

> Can'st thou not forgive the error,
> Wilt thou not recall the word?
> It is little for a mortal
> To be vanquished by a god!

With this beautiful, though not original, sentiment—for it is to be found in several Greek writers—the poem should have closed, but Pater, who was but a tyro in his art, adds some expressions of self-reproach supposed to be uttered by Cassandra, and it terminates feebly.

Upon being requested his opinion, McQueen objected to its sensuality, but Pater, who, though he often asked advice, was never, with his innate Dutch obstinacy, once known to take it, made no alteration; so the lines stand to-day as they were read on that June morning under the tender green of the oak tree in the Cathedral Precincts.

On Speech Day, 1857, McQueen, now in Form 6, carries off a whole host of prizes.[1] Pater obtains the Broughton Prize for Ecclesiastical History, a "Reward" for Classics and a "Commendation" for English, and he and Dombrain get the Tenterden [2] Prizes for Divinity.

48. **The School Speech Day, 6th August, 1857.**

As usual, Mr. Wallace made a special speech to each prize-winner, his advice to Pater being of intense

---

[1] Map Drawing; Classics, English Essay (subject, "On the Influence of Persecution on Religion"), French; Tenterden Prizes, Divinity and History; Broughton Prize, Latin Scholarship; Extra Prize, and "Reward" for English verse.

[2] Bequest of Lord Chief Justice Tenterden, an old King's School Boy.

o

interest to us, recalling as it does Mr. Wallace's fear lest Pater's extreme High Churchmanship should lead him to Rome—a fear which, as will be seen, he, in the following year, reiterated. The good man little thought that there was any danger on the side of Agnosticism and Atheism. "Your papers," said Mr. Wallace, "show that you have studied carefully the history of the Reformation, and it rejoices me to think that haply you may be fostering something of the spirit of that illustrious King's Scholar in whose memory you receive this book. I would that the moral likeness of Bishop Broughton were photographed upon your heart. Then you will be consistent in your walk, swaying neither to the right nor to the left; but, boldly stepping on in the footprints of the martyrs and confessors of our Holy Church, you will recognise in the Reformation as carried on in England the hope of the world—the ark which carries the treasure of the world's final security against spiritual slavery."

To all three members of the Triumvirate Mr. Wallace paid tributes for their diligence and excellent conduct; and of McQueen, the hero of the day, he spoke with warm affection both when giving the prizes and at the banquet that followed. "With respect," he said, on the latter occasion, "to the boy who bore away so many prizes to-day I cannot take much credit to myself, for he is a boy who would have done well anywhere. The only merit I can assume is that of having studied his character and put no impediment in the way of its proper development."

Among the recitations we notice the following:

H. Dombrain	Satan	Par. Lost, Bk. 1.
J. R. McQueen	Hæmon	Antigone i., 683 (Sophocles).
Walter Pater H. Dombrain R. McQueen	Hotspur Worcester Northumberland	Hy. IV., P. i., Act I., Sc. 3.

These speech days "convulsed the more sensitive boys with awe and terrors unspeakable." "My proudest

VIEW IN THE GROUNDS OF BROOKHOUSE,
CHAILEY, SUSSEX.

Photo by Magnus R. Robertson, Esq.

BROOKHOUSE, CHAILEY.

Photo by Magnus R. Robertson, Esq.

moment," says W. K. Chafy, "was when the terrible Dr. Russell caught me, as I passed the formidable row of Dean and Canons seated in front of the temporary stage, with a compliment on my German speech, and Dean Alford said, 'Thank you for making *Lenore*[1] intelligible to one who never read it.'" Chafy, however, gave the glory to his dear master, Dr. Rost, with whom he had discussed the poem in the room at S. Augustine's. The complete school lists for the year have been preserved, and we notice that Henry Best, who had succeeded Philip Duval,[2] was captain of the school, and that John Rainier McQueen was a monitor, while Dombrain and Pater were, as yet, only sub-monitors.[3]

Like so many others, Pater was forcibly attracted by the story-telling power and the humour of Charles Dickens, while the fact that the King's School was the school of the amiable but flaccid Dr. Strong of *David Copperfield* added to the charm of at least one of the stories. With the old Almonry Chapel, the Head

49. Pater and Dickens.

[1] Bürger's well-known ballad.

[2] Duval proceeded to Oxford, and became a clergyman. See Chapters IX. and XXII.

[3] The following lists will interest old King's School boys. The boys whose names are in italics were King's Scholars.

FORM VI.
MONITORS.

James Selwood Tanner. *William Havens Pope.*
Frederick Brisbane Butler. John Rainier McQueen.

SUB-MONITORS.

Henry Dombrain.
Walter Horatio Pater.
Henry William Barber [now Vicar of Ryhope, Sunderland].
William Carolus Bradstreet.

The following were in the
5th FORM.

R. Gardiner.
Robert R. McQueen.
Herbert Macbean Willis.
W. K. W. Chafy [now Rev. Dr. Chafy, of Rous Lench Court].
W. Bettison.

Stephen S. Duval.
W. S. Newall.
C. James.
F. Flint.
H. I. Tanner.
H. Furley.

Master's house adjoining and the Mint Yard in mind, David observes, "I went, accompanied by Mr. Wickfield, to the scene of my future studies —a grave building in a courtyard, with a learned air about it that seemed very well suited to the stray rooks and jackdaws who came down from the Cathedral towers to walk with a clerkly bearing on the grass plot—and was introduced to my new master, Dr. Strong. Dr. Strong looked almost as rusty, to my thinking, as the tall iron rails and gates outside the house; and almost as stiff and heavy as the great stone urns that flanked them, and were set up, on the top of the red-brick wall at regular distances all round the court, like sublimated skittles for Time to play at." [1] Dr. Strong's kindly nature and the love borne towards him by his pupils are suggestive of the Rev. George Wallace, but there are no other resemblances, though the school itself is just as Pater's friends have described it to the writer: "It was very gravely and decorously ordered," says Dickens, "and on a sound system; with an appeal, in everything, to the honour and good faith of the boys, and an avowed intention to rely on their possession of those qualities unless they proved themselves unworthy of it, which worked wonders."

Just then *Little Dorrit* was coming out in monthly numbers,[2] and Pater, McQueen and Dombrain often made merry, as they walked together in the Precincts, over Flora Finching and Mr. F.'s Aunt. As Pater grew older, however, his taste for Dickens disappeared,[3] but he pays a tribute to *Barnaby Rudge* in one of the Essays in the *Guardian*,[4] deprecating at the same time at least one half, on account of its sing-song.

[1] David Copperfield, Ch. XVI., Cr. Ed., p. 179. Written in 1848, it appeared in twenty monthly parts from January 1849, to October 1850.
[2] The first appeared December 1855, and the last June 1857.
[3] See Chapter XXXVIII., page 148.
[4] 17th February 1886.

CHAPTER XV

AUGUST 1857

CHAILEY

All this time Pater, in his anxiety to rise in the school, had been applying himself to his studies far more closely than considerations of health should have allowed. While his mind banqueted his body pined. A thorough change having been recommended, he accepted with pleasure an invitation from Colonel and Mrs. McQueen to pay them a visit at their summer residence, Brookhouse, Chailey, in Sussex. The visit was made in August, and Pater, who, guide-book in pocket, had just arrived from Chichester, whither he had been attracted by the Cathedral, was met by McQueen at Lewes.

50. Brookhouse, Chailey, Aug., 1857

Brookhouse is a commodious country residence of later Georgian date,[1] with stuccoed walls and beautiful grounds ornamented with beeches, firs, chestnuts, sycamores and other picturesque trees; whose leaves in the fall of the year, shed on pond, lawn and winding path, completely cover them as with cloth of gold. On the lawn (which is bordered on one side by a great billowy rhododendron hedge—the rhododendron walk of one of Pater's poems) are peacocks and storks in stone, and the eye takes in many a seducing nook and leafy vista.

---

[1] It is now (1906) the residence of Mr. J. R. McQueen, who inherited it, through his mother, from his maternal grandfather, Rear-Admiral Rainier.

In the house is a noble and wonderfully-carved cabinet [1] which came from one of those old dark houses in the Precincts of Canterbury, of which we have often spoken, while the white marble mantelpieces, and the tall and handsome silver candlesticks which gleam above the snowy napery of the dining-table remind of two of Pater's predominant enthusiasms—whiteness and silver. One room has the original wall paper—hung previous to the battle of Waterloo—the pattern—a noble one, with life-sized figures of jungle fowl—being as bright as on the day it was first unrolled; and among the treasures of the house is a silver and tortoiseshell box brought home in 1798 by Mr. McQueen's grandfather after the capture of the Spice Islands from the Dutch; and there are other reminders of war, chiefly pictures, including one of Mr. McQueen's gorgeous father.

We would not insist that Brookhouse was drawn upon by Pater when he was describing "White Nights" in *Marius* or the homes of Florian Deleal and Emerald Uthwart; still he may have had it in mind. Of the Huguenot ancestry of the McQueens we have already spoken. "The old house," says Pater, "really was an old house; and an element of French descent in its inmates—descent from Watteau—might explain a noticeable trimness and comely whiteness about everything there." White, indeed, is the prevailing colour at Chailey, white walls, white marble mantelpieces, white everything, just as at Fish Hall the prevailing colour is obtrusive red.

Pater's window looked to the south-east and commanded a view beautiful with hydrangeas, silver firs and ilexes. Another window, now closed up, overlooked the conservatory, which has since made way for a more substantial erection.

The god Mars, as we insinuated, dominates the interior of the house, but the roof is sacred to Minerva.

---

[1] Not there in Pater's time.

CHAILEY CHURCH.

Photo by Magnus R. Robertson, Esq.

It is "a court for owls." At night they come out and perch on the ridges, and hoot or swoop down on small prey. They have resided there for generations, and they approve of the McQueens and are of opinion that "all's right with the world"; and the McQueens approve of them.

Pater, René and Robert McQueen rambled together over the North Common—a sweeping upland, comprising even now more than 500 acres of heathery and gorse-clad waste; and when Pater descried from what is called "The King's Head Gap" the distant line of the Downs, dissolved by the quivering haze into a soft blue, he said that it was the sea, and when McQueen corrected him, he, with his Dutch obstinacy, still insisted that he was right. Half a mile from the house is a spacious pool—"the island pond," which at that time boasted a goodly expanse of water, though now it is choked up with flag and forests of velvety bulrushes. On its bank was a boat, and Pater, who had long, as we have seen, inwardly resolved to try his hand, on the first opportunity, at rowing, was convinced that the psychological moment had at last arrived. So he induced McQueen and his brother, neither of whom had ever handled oar, to get into the boat with him; and they managed to quit the shore. The water may have been violet, but there were no angel wings to waft them, as on that memorable occasion when the Celestial Sailors put out to sea. Consequently the boat, instead of going straight on, kept turning round and round; and they found very great fault with it, though that did not mend matters. Presently, however, a handsome old gentleman, named Blencowe, happened to come up, and, calling from the shore, he explained that, if they would pull together, instead of pulling one against another, they would probably make progress. They followed this excellent advice, with marked success; nor did they omit to thank the kindly coach, who had imparted to them in one moment what might never have occurred to them in the space of many years. The three rather terrestrial sailors having reached shore (and very glad they were to reach it), did not during that holiday make any further use of their newly-acquired knowledge; but, Pater, who had, as he supposed, really, at last, learnt to row, was for the rest of the day on unusually good terms with himself. Close to the house is a large barn, often since used for Evangelistic services, and then filled with hen-coops, hurdles and other lumber. Curious to say, Pater and McQueen, who had never played either at King's School or anywhere else, except that one game in the Blean Woods, here so far forgot themselves as to become boys. They began their brief boyhood late, however, for both were over seventeen. McQueen, it is remembered, pretended to be a farmer's wife, and Pater, who personated a sanitary inspector of a very severe sort, ran about finding fault with everything and shouting "What do I see here?" "Another mixen?"[1] "Away with it!"

On the Sunday they attended the village church, a small edifice with a tower surmounted by a steep pyramid, which stands close to the entrance to the grounds. There are several great yews in the churchyard, and when we visited it, we half-expected to see under one of them a tomb inscribed "Emerald Uthwart, born" on such a day "at Chase Lodge, in this parish; died there" on a day "in the year 18—, aged 26." The lads sat in the chancel—which was in those days reserved for the quality, who at the end of the service kept their places until the commonalty had filed out, while the rector, also according to custom, left the church last of all. The edifice has not greatly changed, though a gallery, which looked like an opera-box, affixed to the south side of the church, has recently been removed.

[1] Dunghill.

At this time, McQueen was much absorbed in a book called *The Fairy Bower,* by Mrs. H. Mozley,[1] a sister of Cardinal Newman, and especially interested in a character called Mary Ann Duff; but Pater, as the friends strolled about the park, made fun at the book, jibed at the lady, and laughed down the wind all McQueen's literary theories. McQueen's devotion to Miss Charlotte Yonge,[2] for example, moved Pater to scorn; and he found fault with another of McQueen's enthusiasms, Ainsworth's *Lancashire Witches,* which he considered "very profane in some places." However, they talked a good deal about Mother Demdike and Mistress Nutter—not forgetting—and Pater never neglected any opportunity for catty talk—the black cat Tib. While the lads chatted a number of squirrels, with their bushy tails over their backs gambolled round about, or sat up and nibbled the nuts thrown to them, while now and again one of the pretty creatures would boldly steal up to McQueen and take a nut from his fingers. When dusk once more approached, owl hooted to owl.

For evening amusement Pater introduced a table game which he called Ponchee (with accent on the second syllable)—the game better known as Pachisi,[3] which they played with counters and a teetotum on a board of Pater's own manufacture, made of four sails like those of a windmill, coloured respectively red, blue, green and yellow, and divided into small squares.

[1] *The Fairy Bower, or the History of a Month.* A tale for young people, by Mrs. H. Mozley, London, 1841; octavo, p.p. 386. Harriet Elizabeth Newman married Thomas Mozley (1806—1893) 27th September 1836.

[2] Mr. McQueen thus tries to excuse himself. "If I sinned in this respect, it was in good company; for once when I was staying at Blachford, Lord Blackburn—the great judge—a connection of my host, came thither and stayed several days; and his relaxation and amusement was reading a story of Miss Yonge's, which he asked for; and not one of her best stories either, '*The Three Brides.*'"

[3] It is really a Hindu game. See Burton's *Arabian Nights,* Lib. Ed., Vol. VII., p. 278 footnote. In India it was played on a cloth.

CHAPTER XVI

AUGUST TO DECEMBER 1857

MISS GABRIEL

Among the guests at Barton Fields was Miss Virginia Gabriel,[1] the musical composer (daughter of General, usually called Archangel Gabriel) — a woman of infinite charm of character, who was slightly related to the McQueens. Pater, having shown her a number of his sacred poems, she saw at once that beneath the boy's shy, timid exterior there beat a will that "chafed and fretted and chafed and found no rest";[2] and she made the blood leap in his veins with words of kind encouragement—declaring, for example, that he had in him the making of a second Keble, and that if he religiously cultivated his undoubted talents and used them judiciously, his name would be to after-generations as the lasting odour of musk. Miss Gabriel, who published several hundred songs, some of which achieved remarkable popularity, married, seventeen years later, Mr. George E. March of the Foreign Office, and died in 1877.

51. Miss Gabriel, Aug., 1857.

In the Lists of Foundationers[3] of the King's School from 1751 to 1860, three classes are indicated—the youngest boys being entered as "Prae-elected," the next as "Elected," and the eldest as "Admitted to the year of Grace." The paper is still preserved which gives the names of such as were "admitted," "elected," and "prae-elected" by The Reverend the

52. "Admitted to the Year of Grace" Dec., 1857.

---

[1] Miss Gabriel was born at Banstead in Surrey, 7th February 1825.

[2] Pater.

[3] There were always fifty Foundationers or King's Scholars.

Dean and Canons in December, 1857; and in the first column under the heading "Admitted to the Year of Grace" occur four names, in this order: "Walter Pater, Willoughby Methley, Frank Stock and George Rigden," all of whom had entered the school together in February, 1853. Pater was now studying closely with a view to obtaining the Exhibition of 1858, which would enable him to proceed to Oxford. His mind was, in consequence, in a state of extreme tension, and Mrs. Rainier, with whom, as we noticed, Pater was a great favourite, expresses in one of her letters, written at this time, the hope "that he will get it," and adds, "Nobody more worthy."

To Pater's admiration for Canon Stanley, whose voice and gestures, by-the-by, he used to imitate, we have already alluded. Indeed, he was all praise for the grandeur of Stanley's soul, for his wonderful sermons, delivered with an "earnest, inward, deep-down voice," and for his admirable language both in the pulpit and out of it.

53. The Departure of Stanley, March, 1858.

The Triumvirate had been drawn to the Cathedral even when dull men occupied its pulpit; but a far more powerful magnet it proved when Stanley preached. His sermons continued to bristle with historical allusions, and his earnestness was even astonishing. If he betrayed emotion when referring to a recently-deceased friend, he also had much ado to restrain his tears when speaking of the death of Jonathan; though, as a wag remarked, it might have been thought, seeing that the event happened 2000 years ago, that Time would have healed the wound. His study, where hung, it is remembered, a favourite cockatoo, was often the resort of the Sixth Form boys, whose essays he would look over, and whom he would sometimes ask to breakfast; while Pater and McQueen came specially under his influence, owing partly to the fact that Stanley and McQueen's father were personal friends, and partly to the fondness of both boys for history. In everything relating to the school Stanley took a keen interest, and especially in the play-acting. As Pater says in *"Emerald Uthwart"* the school had always been great "in theatricals from before the days when the Puritans destroyed the Dean's 'Great Hall' because the King's Scholars had profaned it by acting plays there;" [1] and Pater, who was an excellent actor, and imitated to perfection Charles Kean whom he had seen at the Princess's Theatre, once astonished the company and brought tears into the eyes of the ever-susceptible Stanley by his remarkable rendering of a scene in Shakespeare's *King Henry IV*.

Stanley's work *Sinai and Palestine,* the outcome of his travels in the east, appeared in March, 1856; and in December, 1857, he was offered the Professorship of Ecclesiastical History at Oxford. His departure in March, 1858, after seven years spent in "that green island," as he called the Precincts, was deeply regretted by Pater, who, however, though he could not then be certain of it, was himself soon to remove to Oxford, and to come again "under the influence" of his little, but great, preacher.

In the autumn of 1857 the Triumvirate had many "skirmishes" together in the Blean Woods, and on October 12th we hear of them walking to Faversham and back—a rather notable achievement—and conversing earnestly on their way about an event that was causing intense excitement among newspaper readers— namely, the finding of a carpet bag [2] with human remains near Waterloo Bridge. As others have noticed [3] there was in Pater—notwithstanding his sweet-

[1] *Miscellaneous Studies*, p. 195.

[2] Found lodged upon a buttress on 9th October 1857 by two youths, who were in a boat. It contained the mutilated body of a gentleman, without the head. Errington, the toll-gate keeper, remembered that a woman had the night before carried this bag over the bridge, but nothing more could be discovered.

[3] Mr. William Sharp, for example, in *The Atlantic Monthly*.

ness and gentleness—an element of the tiger—of savagery—and a delight in grisly horrors. His mind had a tendency as he grew older to dwell on cruelties, witness some of the passages in "Denys l'Auxerrios," "Apollo in Picardy," and "The Bacchanals of Euripides." He knew and admitted this characteristic, regretted it, fought against it; and in a well known passage in *Marius the Epicurean* he sternly denounces, in whomsoever found, the taste for horrors. We refer to the passage in which he calls the shows of the amphitheatre, the novel-reading of the age—"a current help provided for sluggish imaginations, in regard, for instance, to grisly accidents, such as might happen to one's self; but with every facility for comfortable inspection."

CHAPTER XVII

JANUARY TO OCTOBER 1858

SWEET SIRMIO, ADIEU

BIBLIOGRAPHY :

5. Watchman, what of the night? Summer 1858.
6. Chant of the Celestial Sailors when they first put out to sea. Autumn 1858.

As we have seen, Pater's passion for religion of the High Church type and all its accessories, was altogether remarkable. He was a boy Thomas à Kempis; and, if anything is certain in his life, it is that all this period he was thoroughly sincere. The sweetness of his disposition, his kindness, lovableness, magnanimity, charity, where remarked by all who met him. Indeed, nothing was ever urged against him except by unreasonable neighbours at Harbledown, who would grow tulips in beds over which his cats considered they had a right of way; though it is true that his assiduous devotion to religious observances caused uneasiness to several of his friends, and especially to Mr. Wallace, who, as will be remembered, feared that he was veering Romeward. Presently came a reaction. Owing to the eclectic teaching of Stanley he began to reconsider his High Church position; and the perusal of the works of Maurice and Kingsley, which have had so different an effect on others, gradually led him to become a doubter. He found his faith becoming daily more attenuated. "All my hope in God," he cried in his anguish, "has vanished, all my prayers and mortifications have been in vain," and he shed bitter

54. Watchman, what of the night? Summer, 1858.

tears. Nature by day gave him no pleasure, and at night, to his troubled gaze the moon sank down "pale as a sheeted corpse"; while if he fell asleep it was but to have "wild, weird dreams of grave or shroud." [1] It was while he was in this agonised state, with Apollyon straddling quite over the whole breadth of the way and belching fire and smoke, that Pater wrote two long poems, "Watchman, what of the night!" and "The Chant of the Celestial Sailors when they first put out to Sea," in each of which he exhibited himself as struggling, and not quite despairingly, with his doubts and fears. The first, which is in Spenserian verse and is founded on Isaiah xxi., 11, 12, "He calleth to me out of Seir," etc., opens:

> Watchman, what of the night? So asks my soul
> In whisper'd fear. Watchman, what of the night?

The "dark vested power of night," he says, seems to symbolize the changes of his soul. To him everything looks confused and dim. If there are stars of hope, mists of fear rise and hide them. He throbs with life, yet knows that "the tragedy of death must be faced." He asks "Where are the dead?" A voice replies "Nowhere!" He then remembers that Christ has died, and he implores the blessed Redeemer to hold him from the abyss. It seemed terrible to be nowhere, and he cries:

> Down, down I sink. Oh! let me live in Thee,
> Or deep in hell—it seems so awful not to be.

Presently he recognises that the trouble is within. He calls agonisingly upon Christ, mourns his feeble faith, begs to be taught the way, and prays that he may be drawn, from the mists that involve him, towards the brightness of Christ's truth. "Perhaps," he cries, "all the mysteries of God and man; of feeble

[1] Pater's own words.

man and Him who darkly made him" will be made manifest and clear at death. If it be so, "welcome the hour that lays us in the dust!"—the hour that is to teach that God is both justice and love. Doubts had arisen, but he started back from them "as if he saw his own benighted footsteps pacing lightly towards an awful precipice."[1] Still, his "wondrous appetite" in matters devotional was already (his own words) beginning "to be deadened by surfeit."[2]

The other poem to which we referred, "The Chant of the Celestial Sailors when they first put out to Sea," is lost. It was intended to be placed before the poem called "The Song of the Celestial Sailors" (see Chapter 8), written two years previous. But there was an extraordinary difference in their tone. Then no doubts or fears had assailed him; now he sojourned in Mesech. His religious difficulties and the strain occasioned by his close application to his studies put him into despair; and he felt that death would be welcome. Mournful poems alone appealed to him, especially Tennyson's "St. Agnes's Eve":

> Deep on the convent roofs the snows
> Are sparkling to the moon.

and he would read it aloud with deep feeling.

As his recitation for Speech Day he selected a portion of Tennyson's *Morte d'Arthur*—a poem peculiarly apposite to his state of mind at the time, with its well known line "More things are wrought by prayer than this world dreams of;" but his brother William—now a fine handsome fellow, over six feet, made fun of these poems, saying that he did not care for snowy swards or pale tapers, nor did he want just then to quit "this earthly house."

---

[1] Gaston de Latour, p. 48.

[2] We have given but the merest summary of this poem.

The School Feast Day of 1858 was an occasion of great importance to the Triumvirate; for Pater, by enormous effort, had won the scholarship, and he and McQueen were to leave for Oxford.

55. The Speech Day, 5th August, 1858.

The proceedings lacked their usual brightness owing to a sad event which had deeply moved all Canterbury —namely, the dreadful railway accident, productive of terrible loss of life and limb, that occurred on June 30, near the neighbouring village of Chilham—the King's School "English master," Mr. Fisher, being among the injured.

McQueen had gained a host of prizes: French, Private Study, the Tenterden for Divinity, the Broughton for Latin Scholarship and Ecclesiastical History, and he had various "rewards" and "commendations"; Pater had Broughton Prizes for Ecclesiastical History and Latin Scholarship; Dombrain had only "commendations." The "speeches" that interest us were the following:—

Henry Dombrain. Herbert Macbean Willis Bree Robert McQueen.	King Richard Aumerle Salisbury. Scroop.	Richard II. Act III., Sc. 1.
J. R. McQueen. Walter H. Pater.	Andromache Morte d'Arthur	Il. 407. Homer. Tennyson.

The captain of the school was Frederick Brisbane Butler,[1] a clever, cynical boy, who used to make himself extremely disagreeable to the Triumvirate; and there were eight monitors, J. R. McQueen, Pater and Dombrain being among them.

The Report contained the following: "The Dean having applied to the Rev. G. A. Ellicott,[2] Professor

---

[1] Butler went up to Oxford next year (1859) at the age of 18, and took his B.A. in 1864. He obtained a Post Mastership at Merton, and entered the Church. He was Assistant Master at Haileybury from 1868 till his death 28th March 1883.

[2] Afterwards Bishop of Gloucester and Bristol.

of Divinity, King's College, London, to examine the candidates for your Exhibitions, he has reported in favour of W. Horatio Pater, and the committee recommend that Pater be accordingly appointed. In consequence of the great attention John McQueen has paid to his studies, and his invariable good conduct during the whole time he has been in the school, the committee have presented him with books to the amount of ten guineas.

"Resolved—

"That the Rev. Professor Ellicott, having been requested by the Dean to examine the candidates for the vacant Exhibition and having reported that Walter Pater passed the better examination, Walter Pater be appointed the Exhibitioner."

The Exhibition £60 was for three years at Oxford. At the same time Pater received £30 as a gift from the School, and some friends, whose names we are not to mention, also made him a present in money. After the Prize-giving, the Rev. George Wallace thanked McQueen, Pater and Dombrain for their conduct as monitors, and enlarged upon the good which their influence and behaviour had produced in the school. To Pater he said: "An important portion of your life is closed this day. For the last three or four years you have worked hard. I cannot say that you have been an active monitor in suppressing turbulence and punishing the refractory, but you have always set in your own person an example of good discipline, obedience and order, and ever set your schoolfellows an example of Christian forbearance, a meek and quiet spirit.

> How far that little candle throws its beams!
> So shines a good deed in this naughty world,[1]

and I heartily trust that the good deed of yours which I cannot forget [Pater's magnanimity after the frightful kick][2] may still cast its light and point the way of many

[1] *Merchant of Venice*, V. 1.
[2] See Chapter XII.

SWEET SIRMIO, ADIEU

of your schoolfellows and show them the beauty of that charity which thinketh no evil, and is quick to forget the wrong. Be assured that I shall watch your course at Oxford with no common interest, for I feel that there is in you that which may redound to your own credit and the honour of the school. May God bless and preserve you a faithful member of that Church in whose principles you have been strictly brought up, and carefully instructed, and may He in His own good time fit you to be an instrument of His glory."

We notice in this speech, as in that of 1857, Mr. Wallace's fears lest Pater's extreme Ritualism might lead him to Rome. That there was danger in another direction he did not suspect. It is pleasant, too, to recognise in the speech a presentiment of Pater's subsequent greatness.

Pater and Mr. Wallace, as we have said, had never quite liked each other; but between Mr. Wallace and McQueen the bond had been far closer; and the good old man bade his young friend adieu with tremour and moist eyes. After referring to McQueen's blameless Christian life, he said, "I assure you that with a heavy heart I bid you farewell. During the whole time you have been at school I have never had occasion even to whisper to you a rebuke. Farewell:

> May all pure thoughts
> Be with you, so shall God's unfailing love
> Guide and support and cheer you to the end."

Pater took leave of his schoolfellows in a little monitorial speech delivered outside near the Norman Staircase—haranguing them flamboyantly somewhat in the style of Charles Kingsley at his worst. Among other advice, he bade them "Be boy-like boys," which, coming from him who had never by any chance been a boy, was rather out of place. Moreover, when speaking he looked steadily at Dombrain (who was staying on at the school) and McQueen—which seemed a little unfair, seeing that he himself had, under this head, been the worst of the three. However, the time had come for him to depart. So he bade adieu to conscientious and gnomic Mr. Wallace, beaming and round-faced "Ab," literature-loving Mr. Fisher, erudite Herr Rost, the heaven-supporting towers and the heaven-pointing pinnacles of the Cathedral, the rooks (jet black or snowy white according as the sun took them) rocking above the Mint Yard, the play-ground in which he did everything but play, old Norton's unswerving leg, Mr. Teal's contemptuous lip, Dombrain's archidiaconal face, Dr. Russell's basilisk glance, McQueen's Imaginary Countries (for he still made them, and still many islands and all Argent ruled), the gorgeous figures of Colonel McQueen and other officers strutting "peacockly," pantomimic Bettison, Garter-King-at-Arms Chafy, the old oaks under which he had composed and recited his poems—persons and objects all of them that had become fibre and filter of his existence. Some, indeed, he was occasionally to see again—but with totally different eyes. For the present his religious doubts had disappeared, his mind was once more stayed on God, and every spot round about him had a holy association.

To Pater, indeed, regarding them for the last time as a schoolboy, those tranquil Precincts seemed a garden of piety, pleasure and sweet conversation. "Sweet Sirmio, gem of green and quiet retreats, adieu." Later, as we shall see, his attitude towards Canterbury underwent a curious change. Of Pater's friends none rejoiced more on account of his success than his Aunt Bessie and Mrs. Rainier. Now, thought the good aunt —and she communicated her anticipations to her bosom friend, Miss Ann Pater—now my dear nephew will have no obstacle to his progress; within three or four years at most I shall see him a clergyman, and I shall realise the fulfilment of my most ardent hopes. Mrs. Rainier sent her congratulations through McQueen, and in the following sweetly-sympathetic words: "The successful competition for the exhibition gives her more satisfaction, for her heart was with him, and when she reviews the disappointments he has suffered she is more and more happy. When you write to the Pater you will be pleased to express the same to him, with G. M.'s [1] kind regards and best wishes."

Next day the three friends went to spend the afternoon among the orchis-haunted and scented woods of Blaxlands. Dombrain and McQueen were as blithe as skylarks, but Pater, who had experienced almost more mental strain than he could endure, and whose thoughts were occupied partly with his religious difficulties and partly with the brilliant rôle which he hoped to play at Oxford, was unusually serious. As regards the former he felt that he could say "I have wrestled with unbelief and have come off more than conqueror," and, like others who have passed through "the valley of the shadow," he thought it his duty to endeavour to intensify the religious life of those about him; so as they approached the woods he told his companions a curdling story which he had recently been reading about a miserable man who had died an atheist in the Jesuit's College at Rome—and spoke so solemnly that both McQueen and Dombrain felt that it was intended as a warning as to what might be their end if they fell away from the faith; with the result that they both felt very guilty, though of what, they did not know. Mingled, however, with these sombre reflections were (to repeat ourselves) thoughts of the future; he had been successful in obtaining the exhibition, his foot was firm in the stirrup, and now he would ride, ah, how he would ride! Fame, somehow or other, he was determined to achieve. Wearisome plodding had given him his chance, wearisome plodding might be necessary for the attainment of his purpose. But difficulty, he was determined, should be no deterrent.

56. The Blaxland's Incident, 6th August, 1858.

[1] Grandma's.

After lunch the friends walked and talked together till they came to a field to the west of the house and looking towards the amphitheatre of the Blean Woods where there used to be a fine echo. This junketing, which was necessarily their last re-union as King's School boys, had been very pleasant, and they were just talking about returning when Pater suddenly, and without provocation, gave way to a violent outburst of ill-temper. Though provided with a remarkable fund of caustic wit, he had never before—during the whole of the time he had known them—expended any of it on his friends. The three had never quarrelled, indeed it was not a quarrel then, for neither McQueen nor Dombrain made any retort. The quiet, however, with which they received his biting words only increased his choler, and finally he said in a towering passion, and in an impressive and theatrical manner, "The Triumvirate is for ever dissolved," and stalked fuming away.

That night McQueen could do nothing but worry his wits in order to arrive at the cause of the trouble. "It was certainly no theological difference," he said to himself, "for we let Pater have his own way without contradicting him." Then he wondered whether he or Dombrain had thoughtlessly made some playful remark about Pater's personal appearance—a point that was always a very tender one, but he at last came to the conclusion that the responsibility lay with the nervous excitement brought about by the exhausting preparation for the examination and the ordeal undergone on Speech Day. Next morning Pater, who was all penitence for his treatment of his friends, lost no time in making them ample apologies. He begged them not to think seriously of the absurd outburst of temper, and, without mentioning the causes, which, he said, were not likely to occur again, he expressed regret that, at what might prove their last reunion, he had been so unpleasant to them and the hope that he would soon be able to remove entirely the disagreeable impression.

CHAPTER XVIII

14TH OCTOBER 1858—NOVEMBER 1858

THE EYRIE AT QUEEN'S

Ten weeks slipped away, and when we next see Walter Pater he is at Queen's College, Oxford, and installed in a set of rooms on the third floor of the east side of the inner court, with a sitting-room peering into the dim back quadrangle. He had quitted Canterbury to the sound of flutes and dulcimers as it were, but no one could have been more dismal than he as he descended for the first time from his "eyrie"—those third-floor rooms at Queen's. Anybody might have thought he had just committed manslaughter. In slouching manner, with frightened air, and shoulders more than usually bent, he retraced his steps through the back quadrangle, past the Hall and the Chapel, and through the great Quadrangle into the High Street, too miserable to take any particular notice of the cupola with effigy of Queen Caroline under which he had passed, the arcade, or the architectural features of the collegiate wings that abut on the street. Then turning down Catherine Street he made straight for the King's Arms Hotel, where he asked for McQueen, who, with his father, had arrived there at four that afternoon. McQueen was almost as doleful as Pater, and though he brightened a little when he saw his friend, he expressed with vehemence his antipathy for Oxford and asseverated that he should always hate it.

The college that had been selected for McQueen was Balliol, and next day he found himself conducted to

57. Tears at Oxford, 14th Oct., 1858.

his rooms—two "horrid frowsy little holes," looking out on the street near St. Mary Magdalene's Church and the Martyrs' Memorial.[1] Writing, however, to his grandmother (Mrs. Rainier) on Saturday, the 16th, he tried to make the best of a very melancholy conjuncture: "My rooms," he said, "are somewhat diminutive, but they are cheerful and dry .... the change from home to college has not been effected without a great wrench to my feelings, but I am in much better spirits than Pater, who is now sitting opposite to me weeping. He seems to have suffered intensely, and his sufferings do not appear to diminish. He considers me to be 'the only comfort he has,' and I certainly know not what I should do without him."

58. The Oxford of 1858. The Oxford of 1858, although its main features have been preserved, differed in numerous respects from the Oxford of to-day. Carfax Church is gone —or all but its tower, Brasenose College, after throwing down the row of old tenements that stood in its way, has presented itself with a new quadrangle showing a handsome frontage to High Street, Balliol has shot up an entire forest of gables and pinnacles in Broad Street. The Colleges of Keble and Mansfield have risen majestically, others have made additions of wing or storey or oriel; while municipal Oxford, as its palatial pile in St. Aldate's evinces, has also broken out into architecture. The rest of the city was in general appearance much the same as now. Radcliff Cupola rose above roof and finial. Magdalen Tower lorded it above the leafy, meandering walks by the Cherwell, "the glorious bend" in the High Street was almost the same, with its views of St. Mary's richly pinnacled spire and the façades of University and Queen's Colleges. Peremptory Tom, under his

---

[1] Later McQueen occupied rooms on the ground floor with windows looking into Broad Street and also into the old quad. They were on the east side of the gate-way—the side nearest to Trinity College. This portion of Balliol has been rebuilt

QUEEN'S COLLEGE, OXFORD.

From Photo by Hills and Saunders, Oxford.

Imperial Crown, tolled nightly his 101 significant and unwelcome strokes. The river in summer time, as now, was alive with sporting men, who lived only to put the boat of their college at the "head of the river;" in winter the same men returned periodically from the football field with bare legs and that pardonable pride from which it is so difficult for the University man to free himself when daubed from head to heel with mud. Then there was the extreme High Church set, with hair plastered very close to the head, who spent their money on incense at seven and sixpence a pound, candles and little triptyches with ruby glass doors, before which in sky-blue cassock and chasuble with a gold border they performed such ceremonies as seemed good to them; the extreme Low Church set to whom the nakedness of the interior of St. Mary's appealed; the atheistic set who larded their conversation with all that was worst in Heine; while there were plenty of men, who, belonging to no set at all, preserved in religion a sweet and wholesome reasonableness.

Of individual undergraduates we shall mention only three—A. C. Swinburne and John Addington Symonds of Balliol, and John Richard Green [1] of Jesus, to all of whom we shall have occasionally to refer. Pater did not make the personal acquaintance of Mr. Swinburne till some years later, but he was much impressed, to use his own words, "by Swinburne's vivacious appearance," and more than once remarked on it, particularly one day when he and McQueen "were walking together near Headington and passed Swinburne."

On the management of the colleges in those days it is not pleasant to dwell, for peculation and waste were the rule rather than the exception. The finest of them,

---

[1] He left Oxford for clerical work in the East of London in 1860. He married J. A. Symonds's sister. To his *Short History of the English People* and the fact that he is the original of the leading character in Mrs. H. Ward's *Robert Elsmere,* it is scarcely necessary to allude. He died in 1883.

says Mr. T. H. Green, were the most corrupt, "the functionaries from the heads to the servants being wholly given to dishonesty." [1]

Seventeen years had elapsed since the appearance of the "Tracts for the Times" and thirteen since Newman went over to Rome. Pusey, who was fifty-eight and preached in "a dirty old surplice over ragged trousers" —looking, good man, "as if he needed a brush up,"— had thirty more years to live; Keble, still at Hursley, was sixty-six, and had only eight years before him; Isaac Williams, seven years. Liddon, though only twenty-nine, was already making his influence felt; and his Bible Classes [2] on Sunday Evenings were soon to attract many of the most promising men in the University. The Broad Church leaders, Stanley and Jowett, were just forty. Of Stanley we have already spoken. It is sufficient to add that he loved a good stand-up fight as heartily as Jowett, whom he was always, with his lilliputian fists, ready to second; and that Jowett's cherubic face, never beamed more cherubically than when he and Pusey were heaving rocks at each other, while graduate and undergraduate, arranged as chance or inclination led, flung each his contributive pebble.

To pass from the deafening arena of Theology to the calm retreats of Literature, Matthew Arnold,[3] who was 36, had been appointed Professor of Poetry the preceding year, and his lectures, owing largely to his jibes at the "Philistines" were attracting wide attention. His poem "The Scholar Gipsy," despite its artificialities, had given to the Oxford country almost the charm that "The Excursion" had imparted to the Lake District, and "The Task" to the fields and

[1] The works of T. H. Green, edited by R. L. Nettleship.

[2] Commenced 6th November 1859. Held first in St. Edmund Hall, and afterwards in the hall of Queen's College. See *Life and Letters of Henry Parry Liddon*, by J. O. Johnston, p. 51.

[3] See also Chapter XXI., p. 68.

BACK QUADRANGLE, QUEEN'S COLLEGE, OXFORD.
SHOWING POSITION OF PATER'S ROOMS.

Photo by Hills and Saunders, Oxford.

spinnies of Olney—a charm that was, by-the-by, to be intensified by the publication of the "Thyrsis." [1]

As regards the dons, very many were of the old school—even the hard drinker not being extinct; but here and there might be found a Tractarian and here and there a Scientist. Such then was the state of the University into which Pater—a raw youth of nineteen—had bewilderingly drifted.

Almost the first object that met Pater's eye when he dined in Hall was the portrait of the Black Prince, a student of the college and one of its most liberal benefactors—an object that must have carried his thoughts back to the well at Harbledown and Canon Stanley's historical sermons. From Canterbury, its Beckets and its Black Princes, indeed he was never, as we shall see, to disentangle himself; and he came, curiously enough, to detest heartily all three—city, saint and soldier. Among other distinguished men who studied at the college may be mentioned Addison and Bentham, and, we had almost said, Squire Bracebridge [2] (so real is he) who introduced into his own house the Queen's College custom of serving up at Christmas time a boar's head bedecked, as the song has it, "with bays and rosemary." As might be imagined, Pater's happiest moments were those spent in the chapel, always dark and, on account of the prevalence of deep blue in the ancient stained-glass windows, always cold-looking, with its magnificent screen and its equally magnificent Thornhill ceiling. At first he had disliked his rooms because they were so large and so high-up, but presently he became really attached to them. Bare and cold to the point of asceticism—for Pater's slender resources made decoration impossible—these rooms earned for themselves the name of "the Spartan

59. Pater's Eyrie at Queen's

---

[1] Clough, Arnold's friend, who is lamented in this poem, had at this date three more years to live.
[2] Irving's *Sketch Book* and *Bracebridge Hall*.

Chambers." With his customary industry he applied himself assiduously to his studies, his principal relaxation being a walk with McQueen either in one of the college gardens or into the country. Every day Oxford became more pleasant to him. He delighted in its towers and spires, its ivied walls and its smoothly-shaven lawns; but McQueen hated it more every day, and constantly compared it with "Canterbury, glorious Canterbury;" and if every building McQueen saw was dwarfed, and appeared contemptible, by comparison with the wonderful pile by the Stour, the institutions and customs of Oxford pleased him no better. As for Pater—tranquil and shy, and in the habit of conducting himself towards his fellow-undergraduates, many of whom were burly and bluff North Country men,[1] much as he had conducted himself towards his companions at Canterbury, he was never popular at Queen's; still he was always respected—and in the first place on account of that innate grace of manner which had endeared him to Mrs. Rainier, and in the second because he was credited, to use the words of a friend—Mr. T. H. S. Escott,—"with the authorship of papers crowned with the honours of print"—though perhaps instead of "papers" Mr. Escott should have said "poems." [2]

The Provost of Queen's was Dr. Thompson, afterwards Archbishop of York, and among the tutors[3] were the daintily-dressed "Tommy" Falcon, an expert in Green and Latin verse, the genial and conscientious Mr. Renison, mathematical tutor, the Rev. Edward Moore,[4] the Dante scholar, and Mr. (afterwards the Rev.) W. W. Capes, now Canon of Worcester. Accom-

60. Mr. W. W. Capes and others.

---

[1] Queen's was formerly a North-country College. At this date it was in a transition state, but now it is an open college.
[2] See Chapter X.
[3] There were four tutors at a time, but of course there were occasional changes. Each tutor had £2 10s. per annum from each of the 60 undergraduates.
[4] Now Dr. Moore and Canon of Canterbury.

plished, painstaking and learned, Mr. Capes was called in the college "the omniscient," for, according to report he had read everything and had been everywhere—was indeed a bookish Alexander the Great with no more worlds to conquer. His lectures were enriched by brilliant and attractive digests of the latest works in French, German and Scandinavian literature, "and he had no superior in the art of imparting knowledge." Few, however, understood his worth, so thoroughly did a distant and supercilious manner conceal the warm and kind heart that beat under it. If Mr. Capes made his logic lectures entertaining it was often at the expense of his pupils. Among them was Joseph William Chadwick,[1] "a mere boy—a noisy, gentlemanly High Churchman," of whom Pater observed: "I don't think he understands what the thing means"—and who was specially interested in South African Missions.

"Now, Mr. Chadwick," Mr. Capes said one day, "will you please make a syllogism in one form?" As the youth hesitated, Mr. Capes went on: "Suppose, for instance, I say 'No Missions ever did any good?'"—"Oh, but," said Chadwick, "the South African Missions did do good."—"I am not going to contest the point with you," followed Mr. Capes, "but do put your statement into the form of a syllogism." Chadwick, however, could only fret and fume at the aspersion thrown on his favourite mission, and nothing could be done with him. Another habit of Mr. Capes's—that of making "tiger springs," or, in other words, suddenly asking a man to go on translating—is also remembered. Thus it would be *"Neque vero,* Mr. Pater," or *"Jam pridem,* Mr. Moorhouse"—an excellent habit, though it made freshmen frightfully nervous. Later, Mr. Capes came forward as an author, his books being naturally on his favourite subjects, the Early

---

[1] He became Vicar of Westgate Common, Wakefield, in 1871. He died at Wakefield 13th February, 1882.

Roman Empire,[1] and Stoicism; and owing in part to his knowledge of the most recent archæological discoveries, and in part to his sympathy with the purely human side [2] of the personages described, his text books have the rare quality in works of the kind of being really interesting. Here and there, too, we encounter expressions which reappear in Pater's works, for it is natural that Pater should at times, unwittingly, no doubt, show traces of the influence of his old tutor—his liking for the words "nesting" and "nestlings," for example, being derived from Mr. Capes.[3] Speaking of this period, Mr. Capes, in a letter to the author,[4] says Pater exhibited then few signs of "any æsthetic interests. He seemed more attracted by the thoroughness of German thought than by the clearness and precision of French style, but he was afterwards drawn to Renan."

61. Stanley again. Both Pater and McQueen attended regularly Stanley's Lectures on Ecclesiastical History; they often breakfasted with the little canon and his cockatoo, and Pater took part in his social gatherings on Sunday evenings at Christ Church. Some anecdotes of these lectures have been preserved. Stanley, it seems, liked in the middle of them to cross-examine his audience, generally accompanying his question with a prod from a long pointer. But one day—he was short-sighted—he, by mistake, poked the head of a University tutor who happened to be bending over a note-book. The tutor blushed scarlet, Stanley apologised, and the pointer never afterwards appeared in the class-room. On another occasion when preparing a lecture upon the Early Fathers and Heretics

---

[1] The Early Roman Empire 1877. The Roman Empire of the Second Century 1877. Stoicism 1880.

[2] The philosopher Fronto kissing the fat little toes and tiny hands of the Emperor Aurelius's little daughter, &c., &c.

[3] E.g., *Early Roman Empire*, p. 85, and again on p. 86. See *Gaston de Latour*, p. 1, and elsewhere.

[4] 1st April 1906.

THE CHAPEL, QUEEN'S COLLEGE, OXFORD.

Photo by Hills and Saunders, Oxford.

Stanley asked a friend to make for him a chart of the principal names, and to underline those of the Heretics in red. But the trouble was to decide who were the heretics. The leading offenders "were promptly disposed of; some were condemned with a sigh, in deference to general opinion," but when they came to Origen, Stanley hesitated long. At last he said, "Put a very thin line under him"—"Perhaps," he added, with a smile, "they won't see it."[1]

While Stanley the man was beloved, Stanley the preacher was in many quarters regarded with antagonism—some denouncing his pulpit pyrotechnics, others asseverating that he taught a sort of eclectic religion, which was not Christianity at all, and others that he was going ahead too fast. One of his sisters turned Roman Catholic, other members of his family went in other directions. Indeed, to quote an unfriendly critic, "the Stanleys were always turning something or other, and the public got to expect it of them." However, Stanley has had plenty of champions—perhaps the finest tribute to the value of his lectures being that paid by J. R. Green, who, writing to Stanley, said "I came up to Oxford a hard reader and a passionate High Churchman; two years of residence left me idle and irrelgious . . . . High Churchism fell with a great crash, and left nothing behind—nothing but a vague reverence for goodness . . . . I was utterly miserable when I wandered into your lecture-room. . . Then, and afterwards, I heard you speak of work, not as a thing of classes and fellowships, but as something worthy for its own sake, worthy because it made us like the Great Worker. That sermon on Work was like a revelation to me. . . . . I took up my old boy-dream, history, again. I think I have been a steady worker ever since. . . . Carlyle helped me to work; above all, Montaigne helped me to fairness. But the personal impression of a living man must

[1] *Life and Letters of Dean Stanley.*

always be greater and more vivid than those of books." [1]

62. Pater the Thrifty. After a year or two at Queen's, Pater found his circumstances less narrow, and the walls of his rooms, formerly so "graceless and austere," began to clothe themselves, "though," to use the words of Canon Capes, "the decorative features were used with guarded moderation"; [2] but it is noteworthy that with all Pater's reputation for æstheticism, the equipment of every set of rooms, and of each of his houses was scanty and even bald until the last few years of his life. The admonition of the bursar of Queen's, who every New Year's Day, as, according to venerable custom, he hands to each guest a needle and thread, says, "Take this and be thrifty," was needed by nobody less than by Pater. He was thrifty even to an amusing degree—as persons who have known penury often are, and the habit grew with him.

[1] *Life and Letters of Dean Stanley*, Vol. II., p. 15.
[2] To the writer 1st April, 1906.

CHAPTER XIX

DECEMBER 1858—FEBRUARY 1859

HEIDELBERG

BIBLIOGRAPHY:

7. S. Gertrude of Himmelstadt. A prose story. All we have is a metrical paraphrase by the Rev. M. B. Moorhouse, Christmas 1858.
8. To N. R. N. [JohN RainieR McQueeN]. Lost. 3rd March, 1859.
9. Inscription for Ye Poet's Booke (doubtful), March 1859.
10. Song of the Mermaid. Lost. 1859.
11. Justification, an essay in prose. Lost. 1859.
12. My Cousin. One verse preserved. 1859.

Pater had by this time formed friendships with Mr. Ingram Bywater, now Regius Professor of Greek, and Mr. Matthew Butterworth Moorhouse [1] whom with his habit of comparing men with animals, he considered to look "rather like a lion." In a letter to the writer, Mr. Moorhouse says, "My first introduction to him as a freshman at Queen's was in consequence of another freshman, I. Bywater, begging me to call upon the quiet youth, who, though a year or two my senior in years (I matriculated at 17) was junior to me in terms, and therefore we were never in the schools together. We were together in Lectures, having the same Tutor, W. W. Capes, and sat at the same table in Hall. Bywater, being a scholar, sat at a different table. There was a very elaborate and oppressive

63. M. B. Moorhouse.

---

[1] Afterwards Vicar successively of Bushbury, St. Mary Bredin, Canterbury, and St. Luke's, Bath.

system of sconcing in vogue at Queen's which had been reduced to a most Draconian code of punishments—including even the mention of a Latin or Greek word as a crime to merit the drinking of a quart. I was the only total abstainer in the college, but I do not know how much that had to do with the rebellion which broke out at our table when we found ourselves muzzled in the midst of an examination. Being unable to change the law we determined to emigrate; and as there was an empty table on the other side of the Hall, just under the portrait of Lady Betty Hastings, Pater and I with two or three others took our seats thereat and ordered our scouts to wait upon us there, so that we could quote Latin or Greek to our hearts' desire. The audacity of the move prevented any reprisals, and we were left in peace."

In the meantime Pater's sisters and his Aunt Bessie had settled in Heidelberg—26, Anlagen—and Pater spent the Christmas of 1858 with them; but though he several times repeated the visit he never troubled to make himself proficient in German. Heidelberg, then a town of 14,000 inhabitants,[1] consisted principally of one street three miles long, extending from the Railway Station to the Heilbronngate, the principal buildings being, as they still are, the Church of the Holy Ghost[2] in the market-place, the Church of St. Peter,[3] the University, and the ruined Castle,[4] with its memories of Elizabeth, daughter of our James I. Sacked by Tilly in 1622, devastated by the French in 1674, burnt by Melac in 1688, besieged by Chamilly in 1693, it is not surprising that little was left in the old town to bear witness to its departed glories.

64. Christmas at Heidelberg, Dec., 1858. S. Gertrude.

[1] It now has 25,000.
[2] This church is divided between the Protestants and the Catholics. The two services go on simultaneously.
[3] The beautiful and learned Olympia Morata is buried here.
[4] In one of the cellars is the famous Heidelberg Tun.

During this visit Pater wrote a story in prose entitled "S. Gertrude of Himmelstadt," which contained a song. The story is lost, but we are able to give an outline of it, thanks to the industry of M. B. Moorhouse, who put it into verse with the title "The Rescue, a tale of woman's courage."[1] It was a story of an old castle by the "winding Rhine." A youthful knight who had to go forth to the wars at the head of his vassals, had left his bride, the brave young Gertrude, in charge of his castle. Her presence brightens every darksome room, her confidence gives courage to all about her. If she sighed it was only in the chapel recess; and one object was specially dear to her—a suit of silver armour worn by her husband in his boyhood when "he plighted to her his troth." After days of anxious waiting a runner is seen approaching the castle. "The enemy," he cries, "burst upon us in a wild deep valley. From noon to sunset we made a gallant stand against terrible odds. Our leader then drew us up the slope and we watched and waited in our nest of rock. There the little army —half its roll-call wounded—stands at bay. My chief bade me take a secret pathway and carry the tidings to you so that he may have the benefit of your tears and prayers." Next day the enemy continued the attack upon the entrenched heroes; and just at the time when further resistance seemed hopeless a glorious vision appeared—"an angel form of avenging light." The enemy, seized by panic, fled precipitately, the angel entered the weary ranks of the defenders, and it seemed like rapturous dreaming when the form celestial revealed the face of the noble Gertrude of Himmelstadt. Thus to man contending in life's battle "weary and wounded and sorely pressed" woman hath ever lent help. Clad in armour, the gift of God, and bright with the glory of cheerful faith, she breathes

[1] It appears in Mr. Moorhouse's "Stories in Verse," where acknowledgment of Pater's share in the work is made.

fresh courage into the living and sheds the light of Heaven upon the couch of death. Such, in brief, was Pater's lost story of "S. Gertrude of Himmelstadt." McQueen, who was enraptured with it, said to Mr. Moorhouse in respect to that young man's metrical version, which will be found in our appendix, "It seems to me you have spoilt it, and distorted the points of the narrative." Moorhouse then tried to borrow the story again, but Pater said he had burnt it. "I never grieved more," observed Mr. Moorhouse. "It was the loveliest little story I ever read." "Its style," writes Mr. McQueen, "was very good. Of this I am certain. It was picturesque, graphic, and full of colour."[1] Pater also wrote about this time a number of parodies—his chief butt being Martin Tupper.

It was his frequent boast that he had never fallen in love,[2] and we have no reason to doubt his word, but he felt tender—the next degree—towards several young ladies, including some of his cousins; and his poems of this period were exclusively sentimental. One[3]— and only a single verse of it is remembered—was entitled "The Song of a Mermaid," which commences

65. Fair Cousins "Brimstone and Treacle."

> The crescent moon falls in the west,
> Like a maid that has lost her lover,

and then we are carried to the sea and the crisp cold waves

> Which merriest play when drowsy men,
> Sleep as within their graves.

To which of his relatives the lines entitled "My Cousin" refer we will not venture to decide, but Pater

---

[1] MS. notes in Greenslet, p. 21.

[2] See Chapter XXI., p. 68.

[3] There is no copy in existence. Mr. McQueen gave me the first verse from memory.

was certainly in error in supposing that any one of them had laid a snare for him. He broke out effusively with

> My cousin has a sweet pale face
> And dove-meek eyes,

and then he recorded his determination never to wed, and declared that he was no game "for maiden's wile." The original, however, is lost and no copy has been preserved, though it is remembered that one of the verses was coloured with recollections of Chailey with its "rhododendrons on the lawn." The poem, if we may dignify it by such a name, was for several days a source of much amusement to McQueen, who used to contend that the lady who had fluttered Pater's heart with her dove-meek eyes was not one of his girl cousins, but the mature Miss Ann Pater, of Liverpool. To a Miss Strahan—we believe we spell the name properly—who in 1868 was residing at Bayswater, he was also attached; but, truth to say, his real loves were not modern ladies at all—but marble beauties with irisless eyes and cup-like breasts—dryads and hamadryads, naiads with long weedy locks, and women who lived "in the olden time long ago." Moreover, with his odd looks and grotesque figure he made an indifferent cavalier. His brother William, on the other hand, with his six feet of stature and his killing Lord Dundreary whiskers, took every lady's heart by storm; and he looked particularly distinguished beside his unprepossessing brother. Pater often spent his vacations at the house of Mr. Foster Pater in Lonsdale Square, and, taking a delight in unusual spectacles and anomalies of all kinds—theatricals, shows, celebrities, and especially in popular preachers, he frequently satisfied his inclinations in the company of his cousins. The great Nonconformist attraction in those days was Charles Haddon Spurgeon; while John Chippendall

Montesquieu Bellew,[1] the dark-eyed curate of St. Mark's, St. John's Wood, enjoyed a similar popularity in the Church of England; though Bellew, who had a sweeter and suaver way than Spurgeon, found favour chiefly with the ladies, who fell in love with him in vast numbers. In the pages of *Punch,* Mr. Spurgeon, owing to his persistency in preaching "Hell Fire," was generally alluded to as "Brimstone," while for Mr. Bellew, whose sermons Pater described as an *olla podrida* composed mainly of Mrs. Barbauld and Longfellow, could be found no name so suitable as "Treacle."

[1] J. C. M. Bellew was born in 1824. He was the eldest son of Robert Higgin, of Lancaster. He matriculated at Oxford 9th February 1843, aged 19. In 1845 he changed his surname from Higgin to Bellew. In 1851 he was appointed Chaplain of St. John's Cathedral, Calcutta. From 1857 to 1862 he was minister of S. Mark's, Hamilton Terrace, St. John's Wood. He died 19th June, 1874. Kyrle Bellew, the actor, is his son.

CHAPTER XX

FEBRUARY AND MARCH 1859

BREAKING WITH CHRISTIANITY

It was supposed by Mr. Gosse,[1] and most writers have followed him,[2] that Pater's severance from religion synchronised with his adoption of humanistic ideas—that is to say, shortly after his removal to Brasenose; but, as we have already shown, he began to be a doubter even before he left the King's School, and, as we shall see, he lost all belief by the time he was twenty-one. Up to the year 1859 he had been influenced chiefly by Stanley, Kingsley, and Maurice; and he now gave special attention to the works of the last, who was just in the height of his fame, and frequently went to Lincoln's Inn Square and Vere Street to hear him preach. Though extraordinarily influenced by Maurice, whose sermons, however, he considered nebulous and involved, this did not prevent him from mimicking Maurice's falsetto voice, just as in the old days he had mimicked Stanley. For a time he called himself a Christian Socialist. Some intimation of the state of his mind is conveyed in a letter of Robert McQueen (who was still at King's School) to his brother Rainier. "Dombrain," he says, "received your letter yesterday. Pater seems in a very odd state. Does he still believe in Christianity?" This was on 12th November, 1858,

66. Breaking with Christianity, Feb., 1859.

---

[1] *Critical Kit-Kats*, p. 252.

[2] Greenslet: *Walter Pater*, p. 106.

and, after that, Pater gave his friend McQueen much additional uneasiness. That Pater and McQueen were still very much together is evident from the following entries in McQueen's diary.

1859.—Friday, January 28.—Dies Tristitiæ. I returned to Oxford.

Saturday, January 29.—Pater arrived in the evening and tea'd with me.

Sunday, January 30.—Pater and I went to Christ Church in the morning, and heard Dr. Pusey preach an admirable sermon on Isaiah L, 6, 7. ["I gave my back to the smiters. . . . I set my face like a flint, and I know that I shall not be ashamed."] Dr. Temple preached at afternoon chapel. Pater and Chavasse [1] had tea with me.

Monday, January 31.—In the afternoon walked in Christ Church meadows with Pater, and, returning to the College, learnt some of *Ajax* of Sophocles. Then dinner [at 5.30 p.m.] and some more *Ajax*. After this I went to Pater at Queen's College, and had tea. Pater read his story, "Gertrude of Himmelstadt," written during the Christmas vacation at Heidelberg.[2] It is extremely clever, and on the whole very pretty, but disfigured here and there by the modern Germanised English, and by his peculiar ideas in politics, etc., though in a less degree than might have been expected. I returned to College before 9.

Tuesday, February 1.—Walk towards Shotover and Hedington with Pater.

Friday, February 4.—Called on Pater and dined with Dr. Stanley, *tête-à-tête*.

Sunday, February 6.—In evening drank tea with Pater.

Friday, February 11, at 2, I went to see Pater. Returned to college about half-past 3.

Saturday, February 12.—Pater came to tea.

---

[1] Albert Chavasse, cousin of the Bishop of Liverpool.
[2] See Chapter XIX., p. 63.

BREAKING WITH CHRISTIANITY

From these entries it will be noticed that Pater and McQueen were in the habit of meeting in their respective rooms at Queen's and Balliol, or of taking walks together almost every day; but the intimacy which had been so close was at every meeting getting more and more strained, for Pater had now broken quite away from Christianity, and pained his friend by indulging in "Mephistophelian sneers," not only at "trammelling creeds," but at religion in whatever form, and in attacks upon the Bible after the manner of Voltaire, though many of his remarks were evidently made simply with a desire to give his hearers a shock. McQueen, "unable to convince him of his error," implored him at least "to desist from that kind of talk," but in vain. McQueen then reminded him of their peaceful, happy, religious life at Canterbury; but Pater in reply said, "At Canterbury I was a contemptible hypocrite"—a statement that was most certainly untrue. In the old time Pater had agreed with his favourite Hooker that "Atheistical scoffing ought to be penal"; now, none so guilty as he. In the old time he concurred, too, with Hooker that "all duties are so much the better performed by how much the men are more religious from whose abilities the same proceed"; now, he held religion to be a bar to all progress.

McQueen, who was well-nigh heart-broken, and often mentioned his distress in his letters both to his brother Robert and to his mother, felt that, as Pater refused to stop making attacks on Christianity, the friendship ought to cease. Robert McQueen writing on February 20, says, "I am very sorry to hear about Pater's state. I suppose his German friends do not improve him. I wonder what his aunt thinks of it." We may in comment say that Pater's Aunt Bessie knew nothing of it, and did not hear of his change of views till some years later. She was more ambitious than ever for him to take orders.

Robert's letter was accompanied by a letter from Mrs. McQueen, and on their arrival McQueen wrote in his diary, "In the morning [my mother's] letter arrived, which determined me as to what course I should adopt. So I wrote a short note to Pater, telling him why I could no longer company with him, though he is my sole comfort in Oxford. I went to Queen's College with it and met him on the stairs. I walked up with him and gave him the note, and came quickly away. Thus was his heresy the cause of a rupture which could have come to pass by nothing else. He who for three years has been my constant friend, and in many cases my guide and protector, is now to me nothing but a sad remembrance."

Pater on his part buried himself in philosophy—Heraclitus, Pythagoras, Plato, and the moderns Schelling and Hegel, together with less favourite writers, swallowed up his time; and it was asserted that he used to sit up all night reflecting on τὸ ὄν [1]

67. Maolciaran. The Reconciliation, Mar., 1859.

On February 28th Robert McQueen, writing to his grandmother (Mrs. Rainier), says "René is much grieved and affected by Pater's religious errors, as I dare say he has told you," and on March 2nd Robert wrote to his brother, "I am anxious to hear what you have done with reference to Pater. . . I forgot in my last to add a note to the [Gaelic] word Maolciaran, which I will now supply. It signifies a person bending under woe, and supposed to be applicable to you under the joint misfortune of Oxford and Pater."

Pater, however, wished to renew the friendship, and he sent McQueen on March 3rd (McQueen's birthday) a copy of Williams's work, *The Cathedral, or the Catholic and Apostolic Church in England*,[2] and a poem entitled "To N.R.N." [the final letters of JohN

[1] The Ens, The Absolute.
[2] Seventh Edition, dated 1857.

BREAKING WITH CHRISTIANITY 171

RainieR McQueeN], which unfortunately is lost. McQueen made appropriate acknowledgments, and a reconciliation took place—Pater agreeing never to attack or scoff at the Christian religion when with McQueen.

One of the first walks they took together after the reconciliation was on Saturday, March 5, when they visited Cumnor and saw the ivy-clad church with stump of ancient cross in the churchyard and the tomb of Tony Foster, who, according to the long and eulogistic inscription, instead of being the monster that Sir Walter Scott made him, was a courageous, bookish, melodious-voiced, ready-witted gentleman, against whom no charge could be brought except that he had been known to "twang the treble lute string" and to play the "Italian viol and bow." However, Pater and McQueen talked much about Amy Robsart, Scott's *Kenilworth,* and Mickle's ballad, and visited the meagre ruins of Cumnor Hall—a serrated old wall with a doorway and a fireplace made of wrought stone— while imagination enabled them to hear the sound of the death bell, the call of the aerial voice, and the flap of the raven's wing. Nor did they come away without a sight of the Inn,[1] with its signboard, the Bear and Ragged Staff, and its memories of Giles Gosling, and Michael Lambourne. Equally interested was Pater in the two other unfortunate ladies with whom the Oxford neighbourhood is associated—Fair Rosamund, whose maze is said to have been at Woodstock, and who was buried at Godstowe; and the heroine of the Mistletoe Bough, who is supposed to have met her fate at Minster Lovell.

68. Pater and McQueen at Cumnor, 5th Mar., 1859

---

[1] The original Bear Inn of course has disappeared. For picture of it see *Book of Days* i., 735.

CHAPTER XXI

aPRIL 1859—15TH AUGUST 1859

OXFORD FRIENDS

69. **Browning and Matthew Arnold.** About this time Pater made an honest attempt to understand Robert Browning. "I remember," says Mr. Moorhouse in a letter to the writer, many a vigorous discussion "about Robert Browning's poems, 'Men and Women,'[1] in which I was surprised to find meaning, when Pater professed he could not. He set it down to my having been in love,[2] which he never had been. My knowledge of music also helped me to give him the clue to 'Master Hughes of Saxe-Gotha' and 'A Toccata of Galuppi's.'" Although, thanks to Mr. Moorhouse, Pater obtained some idea of the meaning of these poems, really understand them he never did. We notice that in his review in the *Guardian* of Mr. Symons' *Introduction to the Study of Browning*, he contents himself with the very safe remark: "Music herself, the analysis of the musical soul in the characteristic episodes of its development is a wholly new range of poetic subject in which Mr. Browning is unique." If, however, the poems on music always remained much of an enigma to Pater, not so many of the other poems, of which he often spoke enthusiastically. He regarded *Men and Women* and *Pippa Passes* as Browning's chief works, often called the original edition of *Men and Women* those "two old magical volumes," and always regretted that in

[1] First appeared in 1855.
[2] See Chapter XIX., p. 64.

subsequent editions of Browning's works they were broken up and scattered under other headings.

In the *Renaissance*⁽¹⁾ he describes Browning's as "pre-eminently the poetry of situations," the characters themselves being always of secondary importance.

To continue Mr. Moorhouse's letter, "Once," he says, "Pater, Bywater, and I had a long Sunday morning and afternoon walk, getting some bread and cheese at a little inn, and coming back by Bablock Hythe, when Pater quoted Matthew Arnold's poem, "The Scholar Gipsy":

> Thee, at the ferry, Oxford riders blithe,
> Returning home on summer nights, have met,
> Crossing the stripling Thames at Bablock-hythe,
> Trailing in the cool stream thy fingers wet,
> As the punt's rope chops round.

Pater's enthusiasm for this poem was caught from McQueen, who, with his intense hatred of Oxford, honoured the scholar "who deserted his college for a free and open-air life of wandering over moors and through forests." Mr. McQueen has, indeed, life through been a Scholar-Gipsy himself, shunning the city's din, and delighting in remote and sequestered country villages and the company of husbandmen and sailors. His interest in Arnold began and ended with "The Scholar Gipsy," but Pater and Moorhouse went eagerly to hear Arnold's lectures on Poetry,⁽²⁾ and enjoyed both the lecturer's "impudence" (or "invincible *insouciance*,"⁽³⁾ as Arnold himself called it) and his onslaught on the Philistines. Moreover, we presently find Pater adding to his Olympus, which

---

⁽¹⁾ *Renaissance*, p. 214. Pater and Oscar Wilde often discussed Browning together, and the reader would do well to read the reference to Browning in Wilde's delightful essay *The True Function of Criticism*.

⁽²⁾ Matthew Arnold was elected Professor of Poetry at Oxford in 1857.

⁽³⁾ After his marriage Arnold wrote of his wife: "You'll like her; she has all my graces, and none of my airs." It has been rightly said of Arnold that he went through life with "head erect and jaunty confident pace," or, as J. A. Symonds said, "with that touch of arrogance which nobody minded in him."

had previously been occupied only by Wordsworth, Arnold's two other great gods Goethe and Sénancour; while he studied more than ever his large copy of Wordsworth and read it in his eyrie aloud, and with feeling to McQueen's entirely patient but unsympathetic ears. The aims of Pater, henceforward, bore some resemblance to those of Arnold, but while Arnold stood for "sweetness and light," Pater advocated "sweetness and shade"—the dim, the dusky, the subdued.

Other friends of Pater's at this period were J. W. Hoole and Robert Henry Wood,[1] "Byronic Wood," as he was sometimes called, son of the celebrated singer. At the Easter vacation Pater, Hoole, Wood, and Moorhouse, and one other stayed up in Oxford together. Being the only men left in college, they dined in each others rooms, and had much animated discussion over Darwin and other rising writers. One day they ventured on a "four" up to Godstow. Moorhouse, who, in his own words, "was the only one who knew much about rowing," was stroke; and Pater, who "knew nothing," notwithstanding his coaching at Chailey, was put into the stern sheets as cox—and an admirable one he would have proved had not other crews and the river banks kept constantly getting in the way. He really required a sheet of water about the width of the Atlantic to do himself justice. After countless perils they brought their boat back safely, and, what is more remarkable—by water too—to Folly Bridge, whence they returned to their rooms with raised chins and the enviable feelings inseparable from those who have done deeds of daring.

70. Hoole and Wood, Apr., 1859.

Hoole, who was working for a Fellowship examination and had fallen into a nervous state through over work and ill-health, used to beg Pater

[1] Robert Henry Wood, eldest son of Joseph Wood of Woolley, near Sandal Magna, Yorkshire. Queen's College. Matric. 5th February 1857. B.A. and M.A. 1865.

OXFORD FRIENDS

and Moorhouse, who was then preparing for Moderations,[1] to join him at whist, as he could not bear any conversation. "It was the first and last time," says Mr. Moorhouse, "I ever played cards—having been brought up in a Puritan horror of them. I therefore knew nothing whatever of the game, and had to be told everything by Pater, who was my partner." Though Pater had by this time abandoned religion he occasionally attended services, and took part in various other Christian gatherings. Thus on Good Friday morning, 22nd April, 1859, he, Wood and Moorhouse accompanied Hoole to a meeting of the Oxford Anti-Mendicity Society, of which Hoole had been asked to take charge that evening. There were numbers of tramps to be relieved—each with his tale of woe, from the usual poor, honest, unfortunate sea-faring man with only two legs, to the usual distressed out-of-work with a numerous family dependent upon him, the eldest being not more than a year old. The four youths listened to the various tales of woe, emptied their pockets to supplement the money given by the Society, superintended the supper, and read prayers with the men. Hoole, who was a very intimate friend of Pater's and seems to have had something to do with Pater's changed attitude towards religion, had literary tastes, and one day Pater told McQueen, with great solemnity, that Hoole had now formed a Theory of the Gospels. Pater did not say what this Theory was, and Hoole died shortly after.

As the following entries in his diary show, McQueen continued as much in Pater's company as ever:—

Friday, May 6.—I arrived at Oxford from Canterbury. [71. Commemoration Day, 1859.]

Sunday May 8.—I heard Bampton Lecture in the morning and Dr. Moberley[2] in afternoon. I tea'd with Pater.

[1] He obtained a Second Class 1859.
[2] Afterwards Bishop of Salisbury.

Wednesday, May 11.—I walked about Christ Church meadows with Pater.

Thursday, May 12.—I walked with Pater towards Godstowe.

Sunday, May 15.—I heard a Bampton Lecture and walked with Pater.

Next day the friends took a stroll in the Magdalen Walks, a favourite haunt of McQueen's, because the thick branches shut out the view of "hated Oxford," and admired the fritillaries or snakes' heads, to which Pater so graphically alludes in *Emerald Uthwart*,—"that strange remnant just here of a richer extinct flora," in colour "like rusted blood, as if they grew from some forgotten battlefield."

Commemoration Day having drawn near, McQueen's father, mother and brother paid a visit to Oxford, and Pater and McQueen found rooms for them near Carfax. On Sunday evening, with a throng of other people, they paraded the Long Walk in Christ Church Meadows; and during the week the McQueens lunched with Lord Goschen and other notables at Oriel, and attended a garden party at Worcester College, and a ball given by the Freemasons. On Commemoration Day Pater and McQueen went with the crowd to the Sheldonian Theatre to hear the prize essays and poems read, and to see the Honorary degrees conferred. As usual the building was thronged by dons, ladies and undergraduates—the witticisms of the last, who occupied the gallery, being of the usual type. "Cheers for the ladies in green" provoked much merriment, while "cheers for the ladies in red" literally convulsed the house. Portly old dons who had heard the same jokes for forty years in succession, rocked with laughter; and admiring sisters and crimsoning cousins declared they had never witnessed anything so inexpressibly funny. However, everybody enjoyed it (which, after all, is the great matter)—with the single exception of the irreconcilable McQueen, who "loathed the whole affair."

"The day after," says Mr. McQueen, "to my great joy and delight, we left Oxford and returned to Canterbury, and a few days later we went to Chailey. I don't think my parents could have really cared for their visit to Oxford, for they never repeated it; and I always hurried away home before the Commemoration."

Pater continued to be profoundly interested in the King's School; and several times after leaving it he became Dombrain's guest at Canterbury. Dombrain kept him well informed as to what was going on, and in the middle of 1859 sent word of the romantic event which brought about the resignation of the Rev. George Wallace. In 1856, as we have seen, the Rev. Philip Menzies Sankey had been presented to the living of Highclere in Hampshire. In 1859 the adjacent valuable living of Burghclere [1] in the same county was vacant; and Lord Carnarvon, its patron, observed to Mr. Sankey that he did not know upon whom to bestow it. "Why not," said Mr. Sankey, "give it to my old master?" and he spoke in such high terms of Mr. Wallace, that to Mr. Wallace, though Lord Carnarvon had never before heard of him, the living was given. In his farewell address, delivered at the King's School Feast Day, 11th June, 1859, Mr. Wallace set before his old pupils the principles which had always guided him, and which we have already given. He begged them to have implicit trust in the goodness of God. "There is not here," he said, "there cannot be anywhere—one who has what is termed less interest in the church than had I when I adopted the sacred office as the profession of my life." The Rev. E. H. Woodall observed that it was not often a pupil had the opportunity of returning the debt of obligation he was under to his master. "I must have been," said Mr. Sankey, "the most ungrateful wretch alive, if, considering my indebtedness to Mr. Wallace,

72. The Romance at the King's School, 11th June, 1859.

[1] Worth about £1,000 a year.

I had neglected any opportunity of advancing Mr. Wallace's temporal interests.

Characteristically, Mr. Wallace took as his farewell words the passage from Milton's *Comus,* commencing:

> Now my task is smoothly done.

He was succeeded as Head Master by the Rev. John Mitchinson, who subsequently became Bishop of Barbadoes, and is now Master of Pembroke College, Oxford.

73. At Heidelberg again. Worms and Spires, July to Sept., 1859.

In July Pater was at Heidelberg again; and he accompanied his sisters on various excursions. The object of one of them was to see Worms and Spires. They went partly on foot, partly by rail, and partly "in a most eccentric conveyance known as the 'post.'" They saw much that was interesting and beautiful, quaint old village churches and ruined castles, and they ascended the Melibocus, about 1700 feet, the highest point in the Odenwald. Pater found Worms a dull quiet old town, "ancient but not venerable." From a guide-book which he purchased he discovered the church to be 470 feet long—a statement which he accepted—but another statement which he found there—namely, that the style is Byzantine he controverted, declaring it to be Romanesque. From Worms they went on to Spires, a dull place in which nothing really interested him except the Cathedral—but he was amused at the manner in which the town was lighted—namely, by lamps suspended over chains stretched across the streets. The western front of the Cathedral, restored and practically rebuilt, by the devout Louis of Bavaria, put him into ecstasies; he stood spell-bound before its exquisite carving and statuary. For weeks after, he carried in his mind pictures of the eight statues of the early Emperors in purest white marble standing in niches all diapered with gold; he tried to describe to McQueen the burst of colour that met his eye when he entered the Cathedral, and he declared the whole church to be one of the most touching examples of Roman ceremonialism in existence.

CHAPTER XXII

15TH AUGUST 1859—CHRISTMAS 1859

REV. E. H. WOODALL GOES OVER TO ROME
15TH AUGUST 1859

BIBLIOGRAPHY:

13. The Acorn. Written in an album at Heidelberg, October 1859.
14. The Fan of Fire. November 1859.

An event now occurred which created extraordinary stir at Canterbury and much comment among the Triumvirate, namely, the admission of the Rev. Edward Harrison Woodall (and his influence over Pater will be remembered) into the Church of Rome, which took place at Paris on Monday, August 15; and next day he wrote an affecting letter bidding adieu to his congregation. It was the Grand Cricket Week at Canterbury; but the talk was more of the claims of the rival churches than of batting or bowling averages. On August 27th Mr. Woodall's pulpit was occupied by the Rev. J. B. Kearney,[1] who preached from S. Luke xi., 27. He said: "This is the most painful occasion on which I ever had to preach in my life. On leaving the Cathedral on Friday morning, I learnt with the deepest possible regret of the event which has just occurred. I have chosen the words of our text because I have reason to believe that the question of the worship of the Virgin Mary had a great deal deal to do with the recent event." Mr. Kearney's emotion, the earnestness of his words, and the remembrance of the esteem in which Mr. Woodall had been held excited the audience even to tears and sobs. Dombrain, devoted as he had been to Mr. Woodall, and

74. The Rev. E. H. Woodall goes over to Rome, 15th Aug., 1859.

[1] See Chapter XIII., p. 45.

deep as had been his indebtedness to him, immediately "renounced" him. This may seem a curious expression to use in reference to the action of a boy of seventeen, but it is the correct one. Life through, as we shall see,[1] Dombrain was always "renouncing" somebody or other. Mr. Woodall being of Exeter College, Oxford, Dombrain, who was intended for Exeter, at once resolved that he could not go there. "I could not think," he told Pater, "of going to Oxford under the auspices of a Roman Catholic." — This, Pater considered to be flaming folly, and when he met Dombrain and McQueen at Canterbury in the following December he expressed the hope that Dombrain would by no means give up Exeter. "I neither pity nor blame Mr. Woodall," he said, "it certainly was the right thing to do."

Dombrain, as we have seen, "renounced" Mr. Woodall. McQueen was deeply grieved, though his regard for his old friend remained unchanged, while Pater approved of the step; and this was just what might have been anticipated from their respective characters.

It was during this visit to Heidelberg that Pater wrote in a German Album the lines entitled "The Acorn." He speaks of the acorn deep in virgin soil sending up its shoot and growing into a noble oak; and he prays that the owner of the book may thrive and prosper in the same manner, seeing that all duty consists in grappling with chance and circumstance and in not being satisfied with anything short of victory—until

75. **The Acorn, Oct., 1859.**

> All the forces of thy soul
> Be moulded to a perfect whole.

Then, while all around is whirled and tempest-tost he will still be a steadily-growing oak—a credit to God's universe.

[1] See Chapter XXIV.

Pater nursed the hope that his volume of poems would one day receive the glory of print, but for the present his public was McQueen and Moorhouse; and an excellent public, too, for both of them treasured his work. Mr. McQueen, indeed, got whole poems off by heart, and can repeat—has repeated to the writer—large portions both of those that have been lost, as well as those still preserved.

It was now time for Pater to return to England, but on the morning of the day fixed for his departure he found himself unwell. Moreover, the sky was so brilliant that he felt sure a storm would come on before evening, and he was pressed to stay another day. When, as he anticipated, a tempest did burst forth, he turned the incident to account by writing an idyl, "The Fan of Fire: A Study from Wordsworth." We may notice that one of the poems of Keble's *Christian Year* (25th after Trinity), Pater's favourite book of religious verse, is on the subject of a storm following a fine morning; and as Pater knew *The Christian Year* almost by heart, it may have been in his thoughts at the time. "The Fan of Fire" is a poem of mundane hopes and fears with a secondary meaning. Though Pater had flung aside Christianity, he still, as we have seen, occasionally turned back to religion. He represents himself in this poem as on a hill-top with a lady—presumably one of his relatives—early one autumn morning. The east is like a fan of fire. Turning to her, and, taking her hand, he declares that he is overpowered by the loveliness of the scene. It frightens him, he says. She, too, fears that so bright a morn portends a sombre noon, and tells him that as his way is long, and the winding Rhine by which he will travel "bleak and cold and bare," he had better stay another day. But he does not consent. He loves the earth, he says, her trees, her very stones; nevertheless the scarlet sky—the most dazzlingly brilliant he had ever seen—certainly awes him. More sad

76. **The Fan of Fire.**

thoughts follow, and again she begs him to wait another day. He complies; they spend the day "in home-like talk" round the fire. The whirlwind comes, but at evening the sky is silver-gray, and the poem concludes:

> We walked, we climbed the hill, we read
> Of morn without an end,
> And one sure star. I said "Amen,
> Lord Christ be Thou my friend!" (1)

The society of his relatives, indeed, seems to have had the effect of drawing him again in the direction of Christianity, and his good old aunt, as many a fugitive word bore witness, still nursed the hope that he would take orders.

The weather was still unfavourable, but willy-nilly Pater had now to go, and he returned to England "in perfect loneliness" by way of Mainz. He saw a good deal that was interesting and beautiful, but, owing to his indifferent health, without much enjoyment. In Mainz Cathedral—a huge heavy structure of red stone in the Romanesque style with quaint towers and a lofty dome—he feasted his eyes on the tombs of the long line of Mainz Archbishops, and at Cologne he recalled the fact that Goethe wrote here part of *Faust*, including the famous ballad:

77. **Home by Mainz, Cologne and Antwerp, 1st Nov. 1859.**

> There was a king in Thule.

He found the city itself very dirty, but the beauty of the Cathedral overpowered him; and the effect to his mind was enhanced by the presence of piles of scaffolding. It was the constant presence of scaffolding, round Canterbury Cathedral, it will be remembered,(2) that had so pleased him in his school days. "I have," he once said to McQueen, "a great fondness for a church in progress."

After attending a service at Cologne Cathedral, the

---

(1) Though written soon after his return to Oxford, *The Fan of Fire* was not finished till 29th March 1860.
(2) See Chapter IX.

ceremonial of which enraptured him, though he did not know enough German to understand the sermon, he made for Antwerp, which he reached on Sunday morning, just in time to hear High Mass at the Cathedral; and he could not find words adequate to describe the lofty and elaborate tower and Rubens's paintings.

After a tempestuous sea-passage and an uneventful train journey he reached Oxford, where he found waiting him a letter with the information that McQueen, whose eyes were weak, intended to miss the term. "I missed more than one term," observed Mr. McQueen to the writer, "in consequence of the weakness of my eyes, and this, owing to my perpetual dislike of Oxford, I was glad enough to do, though it prolonged my University career."

78. Back at Oxford.

Pater found his college very full, the number of freshmen that term having been exceptionally large, and he made some new friends, including Thomas Joseph Berwick,[1] a lame man, with a quiet and engaging manner; Oswald Joseph Reichel;[2] Edward Frederick Grenfell[3] from Rugby, and Augustus Beauchamp Northcote, "a venerable personage," devoted to natural science, who fitted up one of his apartments as a laboratory.[4]

He took walks with Herbert Macbean Willis,[5] whom

[1] He took Holy Orders, and became Headmaster of Buntingford Grammar School 1874.

[2] Reichel (Oswald J.) of Ockbrook, Derby. Brasenose Matric. 24th June 1859. Scholar Queen's 1859 to 1864. Vicar of Sparshott, Berks, 1869 to 1886. For list of works see Crockford. Now of A la Ronde, near Lympston, Exeter.

[3] Grenfell (Edward Frederick). Matriculated 1859. Scholar Queen's College 1859—1863. Died 29th December 1870. See Rugby School Reg.

[4] Northcote (Augustus Beauchamp), Queen's Coll. Mat. 1859. Lecturer in Natural Science, Exeter Coll. Died 28th December 1859. Northcote and his friend Tidy were what Oxford called "Stinks men." Tidy (Thomas Meymott), Queen's, Mat. 1859. Vicar of St. Clement's, City Road, London, 1876—1885.

[5] H. M. Willis, a King's School boy, friend of Robert McQueen. See Chapter XII.

HENRY DOMBRAIN,
AT THE AGE OF 23.
Photo by Drayson, Canterbury.

J. RAINIER McQUEEN,
AT THE AGE OF 25.
Photo by Miss D. Blencowe, 1865.

THE REV. E. H. WOODALL 187

he found very happy and very lazy; and one day while Willis was chatting with him in the eyrie at Queen's two other old King's schoolboys entered—Frederick Brisbane Butler [1] and William Havens Pope [2]—so it was quite a King's School meeting—and Pater only regretted the absence of his "oldest and best friend of all," as he so often called him—J. R. McQueen, whom he sorely missed all the term. However, he consoled himself as best he could with Butler and Pope, and two other old King's School boys—Philip Duval [3] and Henry William Barber, [4] and applied himself diligently to his studies, especially Plato, which was certainly more than could be said of some of the other undergraduates. The Plato lecturer was a Mr. ——, who, with all his gifts, had not the knack of making his lectures interesting. This, some of his hearers resented, and one of them—a graceless wag named G—— passed a verse round during one of the lectures. Mr. ——, "though it was shocking form for Oxford," took notice of it and asked to see the paper, which was promptly handed up, when it was found to contain the following lines:

> That patient, dull-tongued, plodding ——
> Of Plato's rubbish fit expounder,
> I do not know which is the greater bore,
> The modern critic or the ancient founder.

Mr. —— read, blushed, got confused, and then, without comment went good-humouredly on with his lecture. From that day onward he was more popular at Queen's, and we have no doubt he has often laughed at the recollection of the incident.

[1] F. B. Butler, Captain of the King's School the year Pater left. Merton Coll. Assistant Master at Haileybury College 1868—1883. He died 28th March 1883. See Chapter XII.

[2] W. H. Pope. Matriculated 1859. Became Rector first of Cossington, Somerset, and afterwards of St. Nicholas, Nottingham (1876).

[3] Philip Duval, Captain of the King's School 1855-6. Corpus Christi Coll. He became Vicar of All Saints', Leeds, 1874-7. Died 22nd February 1878. See Foster's *Our Noble and Gentle Families*, and Chapters IX. and XIV.

[4] Henry William Barber. Now Vicar of Ryhope, Sunderland. See Chapter X.

None of the undergraduates seem to have stood in very great awe of the tutors. One young man named B——, for example, on entering for lecture the room of Mr. X, threw himself on to the sofa and languidly put up his legs.

"Rather a hot day, Mr. B——," observed Mr. X.

"Quite more than exhausted human nature can bear," drawled Mr. B——, and he continued to lie in that position during the whole of the lecture; nor are there grounds for supposing that any particular exception would have been taken to his conduct had he found standing on his head more comfortable.

Pater spent the Christmas of 1859 at Dombrain's home in St. Margaret's Street, Canterbury. Canterbury was unchanged. The great Cathedral—with its thicket of airy spires and grey statuary, its symbols, its surroundings—was unchanged; but the Pater of King's School and the Pater of Queen's College were two entirely different persons. He was now (to use his own words) "an enemy to all Gothic darkness, returning . . . . full of a better taste." In plain language he had lost all, or very nearly all, belief in Christianity; yet, amazing to say he still talked of taking orders. He continually treated ordination in a flippant way, and on one occasion, when the Rev. J. B. Kearney and McQueen were also in the house, he said "What fun it would be to be ordained and not to believe a single word of what you are saying"—a remark, however, upon which, considering the pleasure which he now took in shocking people, it would not be fair to lay too much stress.[1]

79. Christmas with Dombrain. The Threat of Kearney and McQueen

Mr. Kearney made an indignant comment.

"I shall take orders," followed Pater, "just before my examination."

---

[1] It should also be borne in mind that he delighted until late in life in making people uncomfortable by similar sallies. See Chapters XXIX. and XXXII.

THE REV. E. H. WOODALL 189

"If you make the attempt," said Mr. Kearney, "I shall do all I can to prevent it."

"And I," followed McQueen, "shall do so too."

Pater replied that he should take orders in spite of them, or of any one else.

The sequel to this episode will be found in a later chapter.

For the present let us say that, although we have no wish to excuse Pater, it would be well to bear in mind two facts—first, that he was only twenty—that is to say, little more than a boy, and, secondly, that rebellion and a tendency to treat religion flippantly were in the air. A number of the fellows, and some of the heads, of the colleges made an open confession of Agnosticism, "a kind of belief that was distinctly aggressive,"[1] and some were avowed Pagans; but one witty don is reported to have said in the Common Room, "For myself I own I have a prejudice in favour of Christianity." Now, with all these influences around him, we submit that it is not astonishing that a youth of twenty, who had already been troubled by doubts, should fall into the error of regarding the Church merely as a shop at which you pay the ticketed price and take over the goods. In short, without excusing Pater, we desire to avoid the error into which, according to Mr. Lecky,[2] most historians fall, namely, "of not making sufficient allowance for the degree in which the judgments and dispositions even of the best men are coloured by the moral tone of the time, society and profession in which they live."

During a visit made by Pater and Dombrain to McQueen's home at Barton Fields, Pater read aloud a poem in blank verse which he had just composed. The

---

[1] My authority for these statements is the Rev. Anthony Bathe, formerly a pupil of Pater's.

[2] *Map of Life*, p. 65.

title is forgotten, and of the poem itself Mr. McQueen remembers only the two following lines:

> Thereat arose a multitudinous flock
> Of eaglets winnowing the airy void.

The friends had much discussion about Mr. Woodall's conversion to Rome, and McQueen having expressed the grief which the event caused him, Pater gave it as his opinion that Mr. Woodall would no doubt find in the Roman Church the peace which he had never enjoyed in the Church of England, and added, "In fact as far as mere comfort of mind is concerned, I consider conscientious Roman Catholics quite enviable." He made similar remarks at different times, and he stigmatised the attacks made in the Press on Mr. Woodall as "virulent, stupid, and ridiculous." He also told McQueen about some of the new friends he had made at Oxford, including George Herbert Durham,[1] whom he described as "of lanky appearance, ten or eleven feet high;" and Francis Allston Channing,[2] "an American, though a gentleman."

During the preceding year Pater read not only a number of the Greek and Latin Classics but also the whole of Wordsworth and Keats, Carlyle's *French Revolution*, several of Scott's novels, including *Redgauntlet*, Mrs. Gaskell's *Life of Charlotte Bronte*,[3] Macaulay's *Essays* and Thackeray's *Vanity Fair*.

80. The Books he read.

"What do you think of Mrs. Gaskell's work?" enquired Mr. McQueen.

"I like it intensely," replied Pater. "The people and the book itself are so interesting. As for Thackeray . . ."

---

[1] G. H. Durham, son of a Nonconformist minister. Matric. in 1859. Is described several years later as of Lincoln's Inn. He died very suddenly.

[2] Channing (Francis Allston), Queen's College. Mat. 1859, aged 18. Scholar Exeter College 1859, Fellow of University College 1866—1890. M.P. for East Division of Northants since 1885. Created a Baronet 1906.

[3] This work appeared in 1857.

"I have never cared for Thackeray," interrupted McQueen.

"But think of his knowledge of human nature, his noble principles, his keen satire—all these are beyond praise. Pray, read him again. I am sure you will like him as much as I do."

"I prefer *Macaulay's Essays,*" commented McQueen.

"*Macaulay's Essays,*" echoed Pater. "Well, they seemed admirable when I read them at the King's School, but now they repel me. I require warmth, depth, enthusiasm; and Macaulay is cold, shallow and nothing of a Hero-worshipper. He is a mere Parliament worshipper."

"And his History?" enquired McQueen.

"I am now reading it," replied Pater, "and so far I find it altogether superior to the Essays."

CHAPTER XXIII

JANUARY 1860—AUTUMN 1860

A STORY OF A MOUSTACHE

BIBLIOGRAPHY :

15. Sonnet on Oxford Life. 27th March 1860.
16. Greek Minstrel's Song from Iphigenia. 1860.

81. A Story of a Moustache.

Pater's extreme plainness—and one of his admirers called him "the Caliban of letters"—was a matter of real concern both to himself and his friends. Owing to his sensitiveness on the subject, he could never look into the glass without a sigh, and he was once heard to say "I would give ten years of my life to be handsome." His friends were equally troubled. They held meetings about it, just as they did to discuss Universal Suffrage and the Eastern Question. At one of these dark councils "Byronic Wood" was ceremoniously voted to the chair, and he had in Moorhouse an able supporter. It was utterly useless, said the chairman, after an eloquent preamble, to sit down in despair, for the case was not hopeless. The question before the meeting was whether anything could or could not be done to improve the exterior of Walter Pater. One of those present suggested a different hat, but this met with no support, for it was pointed out that he might, in his forgetfulness, take it off sometimes—when getting into bed, for example; and a proposal that he should be requested to do his hair differently was also rejected. Indeed, they might have been talking about a girl of seventeen who was on the eve of coming out. At last, in a Heaven-sent moment, Wood exclaimed: "I have it. He wants a moustache. A moustache is the very thing, if only anybody were bold enough to suggest it to him." And he cast expressive glances at Mr. Moorhouse, who, after considerable demur, at last, amid thundering applause, volunteered to do it. Mr. Moorhouse, it will be remembered, had some resemblance to a lion; but though a lion exteriorly, it was with but a mouse's heart that he mounted to Pater's eyrie. However, he broached the matter with so much tact that Pater, instead of flying at him, not only took the suggestion in the way it was intended, but expressed himself flattered; and that was the origin of the heavy Bismarckian moustache that figures so conspicuously in all Pater's later portraits. The suggestion, made at a subsequent meeting to discuss the External Improvement of Pater, that the hunch-back should next be dealt with found no supporters. It was decided to let "pretty well" alone. If lack of good looks in himself troubled Pater, he was also troubled by plainness in others. If a man was ugly he avoided his society. All his friends were good-looking. Plainness appealed not to him, no matter how clever it might be. All ugly objects were painful to him. Even Goethe did not pass butchers' shops more rapidly.

Robert McQueen, writing to his brother René, 26th January, 1860, says: "Yesterday I walked with the good H[enry Dombrain] in the Blean Woods, and found our breakwater [1] very little injured. We thought how the poor Thotie [2] [René] would have enjoyed the walk. The 'poor good' Pater, I presume, has long since returned to Oxford. H[enry Dombrain] says he now writes very badly." On March 13, Robert writes: "Pater must be in a very bad state. What particular religion does he profess to belong to?"

82. "Oxford Life," Mar., 1860.

[1] See § 11.
[2] His way of pronouncing Dodie; which he called his brother, after one of the Imaginary Countries—Dodie-land. Robert was fond of twisting words.

Pater, indeed, instead of keeping to his compact with McQueen, gave himself more licence than ever, with the result that the bond between them became daily more strained. Moreover, he now looked unfavourably not only on Christianity, but upon its teachers and everything relating to it. One remark of his, made after attending some public gathering, will serve as an example. "Liddon was there," he observed, "looking very saintly and very cruel," though nobody else, it may safely be said, ever detected cruelty in Liddon's expression. A little later Pater made the acquaintance of John Addington Symonds, but, though their tastes were similar, they never liked each other. "What sort of man is Pater?" asked Symonds one day of McQueen. "Is he an able man?"

Of the poems written by Pater at this period we have been able to recover only two. The first, a sonnet entitled "Oxford Life," commences with references to the brown hedgerows and furrowed fields with here and there bright patches of green and silver as seen on the road to Cumnor. The Berkshire hills seem to be not asleep, "but intent, as one who wills strongly." Their bold contour gives him ambitious thoughts, he laments the poverty of his life, and finishes with the fine exclamation—

Oh! for a godlike aim through all these silent years.

The sonnet is dated 27th March, 1860. Another poem, bearing date 1860, is entitled "Greek Minstrel's Song, from Iphigenia." Pater also made many metrical translations from the Greek Anthology, Alfred de Musset and other French poets, and every day he translated a page from some prose writer—Tacitus, Livy, Plato, Aristotle, Goethe, Lessing, Flaubert[1] or Sainte-Beuve.

In March, 1860, the religious world was cast into a ferment by the publication of "Essays and Reviews"—written by seven Broad Churchmen: Dr. Temple, Dr.

[1] Flaubert's masterpiece, *Madame Bovary*, appeared in 1857.

Rowland Williams, Professor Baden Powell, the Rev. H. B. Wilson, Mr. C. W. Goodwin, the Rev. Mark Pattison and Professor Jowett—"The Seven against Christ" [1] as opponents bitingly called them. The Bishops in conclave having condemned the work, two of the Essayists, Dr. Williams and Mr. Wilson, were prosecuted, but an adverse decision obtained against them was annulled six months later by the Judicial Committee of the Privy Council. In Oxford bitterness of feeling in religious matters ran higher than ever; but Pater and those of his way of thinking expended their wit on both parties.

Benjamin Jowett, the ablest of the Essayists and Reviewers—Little Benjamin as the undergraduates called him—resided at this time in some rooms that looked out upon the Martyrs' Memorial, and his slight person, immense forehead, cherubic face, "finny hand" [2] and "barrel-bodied great coat" were no less the talk of Oxford than were his writings and his lectures. Since October, 1855, he had been Regius Professor of Greek, which "he taught the University for nothing"— that is to say £40 a year—nor was it till 1865 that, "after much bitterness" his salary was raised to £500.

McQueen hated Oxford more and more every day. He liked neither the city nor Balliol, nor the Master of Balliol (Dr. Robert Scott), "a grand unbending man," nor the tutors. If he went for walks with Jowett it was always with head hung down and in silence—for Jowett practised the Socratic method when in the company of his pupils—and they resented it. He was always "lying in wait for you to say something foolish, so that he could snap you up," and some of his victims contended that he would have deserved well of his college if he had completed his resemblance to Socrates

83. **Influence of Jowett.**

---

[1] In allusion of course to Æschylus' play "The Seven against Thebes."
[2] J. A. Symonds.

W

by taking a dose of hemlock. Sometimes when Jowett went for a walk with an undergraduate neither of them would say a word the whole way—the young man being deterred by bashfulness, the older man by having no butt at which to discharge his wit. It is on record that at the end of one of these silent walks an undergraduate mustered up sufficient courage to observe that it was a fine day, whereupon Jowett snapped him up with: "It is a mistake to make meaningless remarks just for the sake of saying something. Better be silent than cause yourself to appear foolish to your companion." [1] Pater, however, who attended Jowett's lectures, was much drawn to the great man, and it is on record that Jowett, pleased with some remark that Pater made, once said to him, "You have a mind that will attain eminence." Recalling these times, Pater, many years after, writing to the Rev. Professor Lewis Campbell, said:[2] "I received much kindness and help from him when I was reading for my degree and afterwards. A large number of his hours in every week of Term time must have been spent in the private teaching of undergraduates, not of his own college, over and above his lectures, which, of course, were open to all. They found him a very encouraging but really critical judge of their work."

Referring to Jowett's great originality as a writer and a thinker, Pater says: "He seemed to have taken the measure not merely of all opinions, but of all possible ones, and to have put the last refinements on literary expression. . . . When he lectured on Plato, it was a fascinating thing to see those qualities as if in the act of creation, his lectures being informal, unwritten, and seemingly unpremeditated, but with many a long-remembered gem of expression, or delightfully novel idea, which seemed to be lying in wait

---

[1] We are aware that the truth of this story has been questioned, but old pupils of Jowett assure us that it is more likely to be true than false. Besides, who would wish to rob Jowett of his only fault as a tutor—his one ewe lamb?

[2] *Life of Benjamin Jowett.*

whenever, at a loss for a moment in his somewhat hesitating discourse, he opened a book of loose notes."[1]

If from Jowett, as was certainly the case, Pater caught his enthusiasm for Plato; it was probably the influence of Jowett that now caused him to cease writing poetry. This can scarcely be regarded as a misfortune. There is a prettiness and a pleasant ring about Pater's poems, but there is little originality. He lacked fire; and at the best would have made a very inferior Matthew Arnold.

Jowett indeed, whose cold water would have quenched anybody less inflammable than a Swinburne, was never tired of projecting his scorn upon poets, especially of the undergraduate variety. Of one man he said: "He took to poetry and that sort of nonsense." And from his own point of view Jowett was correct. It is not, it never has been, the imaginative men—the men of genius who take the highest honours at a University. Pater himself is a case in point. He was, and always continued to be, from a University point of view, "a poor scholar." Yet when the enthusiastic pilgrim makes his way to Oxford, Pater is the one man among the moderns, that he troubles to enquire about. But if Jowett led Pater to fall out with verse, he caused him to take an increased interest in prose—and to love, above all things, the art of biography writing. Jowett, indeed, by means of his lectures and his writings has done almost as much for Boswell as Carlyle did for Cromwell. He read Boswell's *Life of Johnson* fifty times, and showed that Macaulay had been guilty of the silliest of silly sayings in respect to its author. "Boswell," says Macaulay, "attained eminence by reason of his weakness. If he had not been a great fool, he would never have been a great writer." "Let any one," comments Jowett, "who believes that an ordinary man can write a great biography make the experiment himself. I would have him try to describe the most interesting

[1] *Life of Jowett.*

dinner-party at which he was ever present; let him write down from memory a few of the good things which were said, not forgetting to make an incidental allusion to the good things that were eaten, let him aim at giving what I may call the dramatic effect of the party. And then let him compare the result with Boswell's account of the famous dinner at Mr. Dilly's, the bookseller in the Poultry where Johnson was first introduced to Wilkes, and he will begin to understand the nature of Boswell's genius."[1]

Now, Pater's strength, as we have already remarked, lay in Biography, but Biography of a peculiar kind. He excelled, as we have shown, even from boyhood, in making Imaginary Portraits—sometimes portraits of real persons embellished in his peculiar way—such as Emerald Uthwart, Ronsard (in *Gaston de Latour*), Jean Baptiste Pater (in *Imaginary Portraits*), and sometimes of Ideas to which he gave flesh, blood and motion—such as Sebastian Van Storck and Denys l'Auxerrois.

If Jowett killed the Poet, then, he quickened the Biographer, and more charming Biographies in Little than Walter Pater's surely never were written.

[1] *The Life of Dr. Johnson* . . with copious notes . . . by Malone. Vol. III., pp. 63 to 77.

CHAPTER XXIV

OCTOBER 1860—1862

THE TRIUMVIRATE DISSOLVED

    Having cast aside Christianity Pater now tried to obliterate all his connections with it. First he burnt his manuscript volume of poems—not because he thought lightly of their merits, but simply because of their Christian tone, though it should not be overlooked that he had recently been reading Goethe's *Wahrheit und Dichtung* with its account of a similar holocaust.[1] Pater, indeed, had made Goethe his guiding star, and the life of Pater, and that of the man whom Pater styles admiringly "the greatest of the Humanists," offer other parallels. He did not forget that he had lent the book to McQueen and Moorhouse with full permission to copy out what poems they pleased and to do what they liked with them; nor did he ever request the destruction of these copies. His only desire, indeed, was to remove the sight of them from his own eyes. Next he resolved to get rid of all his religious books—those books on Christianity which he had studied so sedulously at Canterbury. In this matter again he was actuated not by the wish for their destruction, but by the determination to remove them out of his sight; for, as might be expected of so thrifty and careful a man, he carried the more valuable ones to the Oxford booksellers and sold them. He gave his copy of *Augustinus de Civitate Dei* (2 vols.) to McQueen,[2] and decided to put all the rest on the fire, including his copy of

84. Pater burns his Manuscript Book of Poems

---

[1] Book VI.
[2] Who still has it.

Williams's *Cathedral*,[1] which the booksellers refused to purchase because Pater had coloured (and very beautifully and delicately) its floriated headings. Ultimately, however, it was purchased by Moorhouse, who also bought, merely to save it from the flames, Pater's copy of *The Christian Year*—his parting with which shows, perhaps, more clearly than any other action his determination to cleave his life in twain.

Dombrain went up to Oxford (his college being Pembroke—for he would have nothing to do with Exeter) in October, 1860, and took an early opportunity of calling on McQueen and Pater. He had not been in Pater's company many minutes, before all his suspicions were verified; and he not only then and there "renounced" him, but repeatedly urged McQueen to do the same,[2] saying to him, "You ought at once to take this step, unless you wish to be indoctrinated with his principles."

85. The Triumvirate is dissolved, Autumn, 1860.

McQueen, who had long been wavering, now came to a decision. It was a terrible trial to him, but he felt that there was no other way open. So one day in October, in Dombrain's room at Pembroke College, he told Pater with much sorrow that their friendship must cease, and "spoke with him for the last time in this world." The friendship thus dissolved had lasted a little over five and a half years, but the friendship between McQueen and Dombrain terminated only with the death of the latter. Dombrain erased Pater entirely from his mind, but McQueen's affection for him never ceased, and as late as November, 1903, in conversation with the writer, he spoke of his friend with the same tenderness that had characterised his utterances forty-three years previous.

[1] Isaac Williams (1802—1865), Tractarian. He wrote Tract 80, and was at this time living at Stinchcombe, in Gloucestershire. His principal work was *The Cathedral and other Poems.*

[2] We must again remind the reader that we are talking about very young men, almost boys.

THE TRIUMVIRATE DISSOLVED

Henceforward Pater lived in a kind of disguise. He purposely enshrouded himself in mists. "I used to wonder," says Mr. McQueen, "in the later years of my intimacy with him, and when he had altogether ceased to appear as the ascetic and saintly boy of my earlier acquaintance (1855—1857), and I have in recent times wondered yet more, what the real Pater was. He was an admirable (because unconscious) *actor*; and I think an instance of Jekyll and Hyde dualism."[1] In short, like his Denys l'Auxerrois, he had "his contrast"—his "dark or emphatic side; was like a double creature." [2]

Extraordinary to say, although Pater had bastioned himself against Christianity, though he never lost an opportunity of girding at it, and though he had quite lost faith in the efficacy of prayer, nevertheless he still declared that he would take Holy Orders. He still frequented places of worship—though only ornate services with elaborate music and "sweet heady incense" pleased him, for like his favourite Goethe he now regarded religion as merely a department of art.

His chief place of resort of this kind was S. Thomas's —the church of that giant and saint—the ritualistic Rev. Thomas Chamberlain [3]—a man who exercised a lasting influence on many who became acquainted with him. The parish having long been "neglected, poor, forsaken, the haunt of thieves and harlots,"[4] Mr. Chamberlain, who subsequently had the assistance of two well known philanthropic Oxford ladies, the indefatigable Miss Hughes and the holy Miss Felicia

86. The Rev. Thomas Chamberlain.

---

[1] MS. note in Greenslet, p. 29.

[2] *Imaginary Portraits*, p. 66.

[3] Afterwards Canon Chamberlain. He died 20th January 1892, aged 81 years, and lies in S. Thomas's Churchyard, under a red marble cross standing on a rock.

[4] "Felicia Skene of Oxford," a memoir by E. C. Rickards Murray, 1902. Miss Skene was born in 1821. She died in 1899, aged 78, and was buried in S. Thomas's Churchyard.

Skene, and a band of devoted and enthusiastic curates, set himself the task of reforming it.[1] He evoked the arm of the law to suppress the houses of evil repute. He had daily services and choral celebrations, he established a sisterhood and founded a periodical called *The Ecclesiastic*. His tall majestic figure, and his indomitable perseverance in the face of opposition led men to call him "the modern a'Becket," and it seemed at one time as though, like his famous prototype he would have to suffer "martyrdom."

When abused by the rabble he made no retort, when bespattered with mud and struck with stones his only action was to wipe the blood from his face. Then cholera and small-pox broke out in that part of the town, and his unselfish devotion to the suffering put his enemies to shame and silence.

On one occasion Pater took Mr. Moorhouse to S. Thomas's, but the latter likened the service to a dinner served with gold plate and nothing to eat. Next day they attended the gorgeous functions at Merton College Chapel;[2] and, says Mr. Moorhouse, "To hear Mr. Sergeant, one of the fellows, sing 'Is it nothing to you, all ye that pass by,' on Good Friday, was something very fine as a musical entertainment." Mr. Moorhouse, indeed, liked Merton no better than S. Thomas's, and at last he induced Pater to accompany him to some Low Church services. Then it was Pater's turn to complain. "They are spectacularly disappointing," he would say, wearily, or "such starveling ceremonies are really not worth witnessing"; while for the sermons he had no criticism except as regards the language. "It doesn't matter in the least what is said," he observed languidly, "as long as it is said beautifully."

87. Pater and Moorhouse.

[1] See *Memoir of Rev. Thomas Chamberlain*, by Rev. A. Barrington-Simeon.

[2] The arrangements here were curious—the parish services being held in the nave and the college services in the choir.

"The divergence between Pater and me," says Mr. Moorhouse, "steadily increased till one evening I painfully remember when he and another who had been reading Darwin's *Origin of Species* proved with remorseless logic that if God was everywhere—*we* could have no existence at all! I tried to rebut the fallacy, but in vain, and that night, for the first, and last, time in my life, I threw myself on my bed without prayer. I awoke the next morning as from a hideous nightmare, and cast myself on my knees in the deepest gratitude that revelation was as much superior to logic as light to darkness. I told them that we must argue no more on these subjects, and if I remember aright we confined our discussions to secular matters, and there was always a certain constraint from that time forward.[1]

<small>88. Darwin.</small>

Moorhouse, who had been uncertain whether to follow the career of a barrister or a clergyman, now decided in favour of the latter. At Christmas, 1860, he wrote for a Young Men's Missionary meeting some lines [2] inculcating the importance of doing one's duty, and of struggling on, cheered by the belief that "Christ is with every one." He said—

<blockquote>
No lower hope enchains us,
The love of Christ constrains us,
Our lives are not our own.
</blockquote>

Pater, however, on being shown the verses, only shook his head and declared that they conveyed no meaning to him. On another composition submitted to him—"An Oxford Valentine" [3]—he refused to comment—but later he recommended Mr. Moorhouse to "write more hymns." "You really excel," he said, "as a hymn writer."

<small>[1] Letter to me 21st December 1903.
[2] "Lines for a Young Men's Missionary Meeting (held in a schoolroom high up on the Yorkshire Moors), Christmas, 1860." I have a copy in Mr. Moorhouse's handwriting.
[3] *Stories in Verse*, by M. B. Moorhouse, p. 204.</small>

When W. K. W. Chafy went up to Oxford, in October, 1861, almost his earliest act was to enquire about the Triumvirate; and he was thoroughly amazed to learn from Dombrain that the intimate brotherhood was dissolved. "Pater," observed Dombrain, "apostasized from Christianity; and McQueen and I renounced him." To Chafy this seemed "harsh and narrow." But as a matter of fact, it was only Dombrain who had "renounced" Pater, for McQueen lived constantly in the hope that the friendship would be renewed—would, indeed, have renewed it at any time if Pater had been willing to keep any reasonable guard upon his tongue. While, however, McQueen was liberally-minded, Dombrain, with all his high principles and godliness, was, life through, curiously narrow. He kept on all his days "renouncing" people who did not happen to agree precisely with him. Everybody who did not conform to his Procrustean rule he renounced—unchurched—anybody, for example, no matter how orthodox otherwise he might be, who saw good in a Nonconformist; and anybody, too, in favour of more or less ritual than he, fared no better. Amusingly enough, after years of friendship, he at last "renounced" Mr. Chafy—merely on account of some unimportant theological difference.

89. W. K. W. Chafy and Dombrain.

It was the opinion of a friend of Pater's later years, the Rev. Dr. Bussell, that although Pater declined from the Faith, he was never in his heart of hearts a confirmed atheist—that he hung to religion, as it were, by a few fibres, just as—if we may borrow a simile from the country-side—the hawthorn trunks hang to the parent root-stocks after the hedge has been "laid." The idea is a beautiful one, and for those who like to adopt it we may point out that Pater once observed: "Abstract terms like atheism, infidelity—abstract propositions about them make me think of a worn old screw, which turns either way with equal facility and compacts

THE TRIUMVIRATE DISSOLVED

nothing." However that may be, and whatever Pater's inmost thoughts, it is certain that to all outward appearance he was entirely severed from religion.

Hitherto Pater had generally stayed during his Easter and Christmas vacations with his uncle Foster Pater in Lonsdale Square, Islington, but the Christmas of 1861 he spent with his cousin Ann at Liverpool.

CHAPTER XXV

OCTOBER 1862 TO FEBRUARY 1864

THE FINAL EXAM.; AND MCQUEEN'S LETTER TO THE BISHOP OF LONDON

Pater sat for his final examination in the Michaelmas term of 1862, but obtained only a Second Class Honours in Literæ Humaniores. The "painful duty" of communicating to him the result devolved upon Moorhouse. Says Mr. Moorhouse, "I had an idea that it would lessen the bitterness if he heard my slow steps on the stairs, but I only got a severe scolding for not telling him sooner." The same cause—that is to say, Pater's attitude towards religion—that had broken up the Triumvirate now began to tell on the comradeship of Pater and Moorhouse; but the connection was not quite severed, for they [1] corresponded for many years, and Mr. Moorhouse never after visited Oxford without calling on his old friend.

90. The Final Exam.

McQueen wrote a note to Pater congratulating him on his Honours, and Pater, in a letter of thanks made a curious allusion to their friendship "in what is now a good many years ago"—though in reality it was only two and a half years. McQueen and Pater appeared on the same day (11th December, 1862),[2] before the Vice-Chancellor to take their degrees; but though they saw each other, they had no opportunity of exchanging a word.

[1] Mr. Moorhouse left Oxford in 1863, having been appointed to the curacy of Tintwistle, in Cheshire.

[2] "In a congregation held on Thursday, December 11, the following degrees were confirmed: John Rainier McQueen (Balliol), Walter Horatio Pater (Queen's)," &c., &c.—*Oxford Chronicle.*

THE FINAL EXAMINATION

The day after taking his degree, McQueen returned to Chailey, and a little later the news came that Pater was seeking ordination at the hands of the Bishop of London (Archibald Campbell Tait, afterwards Archbishop of Canterbury). Dombrain at once informed the Rev. John Bachelor Kearney and McQueen, who the same day wrote to Pater, and begged him to give up the idea while in his state of unbelief. "For your own sake," he said, "I ought to oppose you."

91. McQueen's Letter to the Bishop of London, Dec., 1862.

Receiving no reply, McQueen, who was greatly troubled, then wrote to (Canon) Liddon,[1] feeling sure that Liddon, who took an interest in Pater and was kindly disposed towards him, would be the best person to consult. He explained precisely how matters stood and concluded his letter with "What shall I do?"

Liddon, who was also deeply moved, replied at once, "Write to the Bishop of London. You might be able to prevent ordination, and if not you will have delivered your soul."[2]

McQueen, thereupon, wrote to the Bishop (December, 1862).

"I knew," says Mr. McQueen, "that by thus writing I should lose all chance of recovering Pater's friendship, and that I should probably lose the friendship of Dr. Stanley, who, as an extremely broad Churchman and great friend of Jowett, who was then taking so keen an interest in Pater, would almost certainly disapprove of what I did. I was very sorry to take this course, but I thought, and am still convinced, that I was doing my duty." The Rev. J. B. Kearney also wrote to the Bishop of London in the same strain, and as a result Pater was prevented from taking orders.

[1] At this time Vice-Principal of S. Edmund Hall, Oxford. He became Canon of St. Paul's, London, in 1870.

[2] Ezekiel XXIII., v. 9. "Nevertheless, if thou warn the wicked of his way to turn from it; if he do not turn from his way, he shall die in his iniquity; but thou hast delivered thy soul."

No more letters passed between McQueen and Pater; and McQueen, for whatever reason, never had further communication with Dr. Stanley. Bitter as Pater was at the moment against McQueen, he ultimately came to recognise that his old friend had acted righteously, and he always looked back upon this painful incident with regret. We can, indeed, imagine him recalling it with a pang when he wrote that passage in *The Guardian* about the doubts and troubles of Robert Elsmere. "A man," he says, "such as Robert Elsmere came to be, ought not to be a clergyman of the Anglican Church. . . . . Doubtless, it is part of the ideal of the Anglican Church that, under certain safeguards, it should find room for latitudinarians even among its clergy. Still, with these, as with all other genuine priests, it is the positive, not the negative, result that justifies the position." [1]

With this incident, the Rev. J. B. Kearney passes out of Pater's life. He subsequently became Assistant Master of Bishop Stortford Grammar School (1862-3), Curate of S. Paul's, Fareham, 1865-6, of Shrivenham 1866, Vicar of Bourton 1867-1899, and he now resides at Cambridge.

After leaving Oxford, McQueen visited Shetland, where, chiefly, it would seem, for sentiment, he purchased an estate; but he resided principally at Chailey. As for Pater, though naturally chagrined at first in being thwarted in his desire, he made no special trouble of it, and—the Church being closed to him—he delivered himself body and soul to the ambition of his boyhood—making henceforward success in literature his one and solitary aim. But for McQueen's letter, indeed, he would probably have been buried for life in some out-of-the-way English village, where, cut off from the influences that made his books possible—the influences of A. C. Swinburne, Richard Robinson, Richard C. Jackson and others, he would never have arrived at the

[1] *The Guardian*, 28th March 1888.

THE FINAL EXAMINATION

goal towards which he so ardently strove—the magnificent goal of Fame.

Of some assistance to Pater was an essay society—The Old Mortality [1]—to which he was elected in 1863, and which included among its members Ingram Bywater, T. H. Green, Henry Nettleship, Alfred Robinson, Edward Bryce and Edward Caird; and it was at one of its gatherings that he first met Mr. A. C. Swinburne. Like the other members he contributed essays, one of them being a sort of philosophical "hymn of praise to the Absolute."

Up to the moment of Pater's taking his degree, his Aunt Bessie, who was still in Germany with his sisters, nursed the hope that he would become a clergyman. Of his multitudinous religions and states of mind since he left Canterbury, she knew nothing; and when she saw him after he had taken his degree she asked anxiously: "Walter, when are you going to be ordained?"

92. Death of Aunt Bessie, 1863.

"Never," he replied. "My opinions are changed." To the poor lady who, of course, could not foresee that her nephew's exclusion from Holy Orders was the very best occurrence possible for him, the news proved a terrible shock. All the hopes of a lifetime were in a moment shattered, and for the rest of her days which, however, were but few, she made a trouble of it.

Pater, as usual, spent the Easter Vacation [1863] with his Uncle Foster in Lonsdale Square, Islington. The year was a joyous one for the country on account of the marriage of the Prince of Wales, but it was a sad one for Pater, for, while he stayed with his cousins, came news of the death of his Aunt Bessie, which took place at Dresden,[2] where she was residing with her nieces. Walter, who was deeply troubled, for his aunt had been very dear to him—had, indeed, given up her whole life

[1] It flourished between 1858 and 1865.
[2] She was buried at Dresden, and there is a stone to her memory.

for her nephews and nieces, at once started for Dresden, whence, after performing the sad duties that devolved upon him, he returned, bringing his sisters with him to Lonsdale Square.

On his arrival at Oxford he found the battle between High Church and Broad Church still proceeding furiously—the question of the moment being whether the degree of D.C.L. should or should not be conferred on Kingsley. High Church, led by Pusey, held up its pious hands in horror, screamed "Hypatia!" till it was purple in the face, and said it had never picked up an uncleaner book; while Broad Church complained holily of High Church's coarse language. All this, however, affected Pater considerably less than the news that his old friend Canon Stanley was to be promoted to the Deanery of Westminster, and to be married to Lady Augusta Bruce. "Let us hope," commented a friend of Stanley's, "that he won't get hold of an interesting book about Becket or the Black Prince on the morning of the marriage, or he'll forget to put in an appearance."

CHAPTER XXVI

5TH FEBRUARY 1864—FEBRUARY 1866

THE CRYSTAL MAN

BIBLIOGRAPHY :

17. Diaphanéité. MS. dated 1864.
18. Coleridge. *Westminster Review*, January 1866.

In 1864 Pater was fortunate enough (thanks chiefly, it is said, to his knowledge of German philosophy, and especially of the systems of Schelling and Hegel) to gain a Fellowship at Brasenose, and the entry in the Vice-President's Register recording his election runs as follows :—   93. Probationary Fellow of Brasenose.

"February 5, 1864.

A Fellowship, vacant by the resignation of Mr. C. J. Wood, M.A., on the original Foundation having been duly advertised, twelve candidates presented themselves, when Mr. Walter Horatio Pater, B.A., of Queen's College, was elected Probationary Fellow *per maximam partem suffragentium.*" [1]

It was a Classical Fellowship.

The election of Mr. John Davis Davenport, B.A.,[2] to a Mathematical Fellowship in the same college is also recorded.

---

[1] This entry was kindly given to me by Pater's friend, the Rev. Dr. Bussell.

[2] Mr. J. D. Davenport never resided in College. At the end of the year of probation, work was found for Pater, but not for Davenport, who then left Oxford and went to the Bar. He remained a Fellow till 1875 or 1876, vacating his Fellowship on marriage. Mr. Davenport now resides at 17, Kensington Park Gardens, London, W.

Pater was twenty-four. He was a happy man in the sense that he had fallen into precisely the niche that was most suited for his peculiar genius. His life hitherto had brimmed with anxieties. Poverty had daily dogged his footsteps, but at last, after his long voyage over stormy seas, he had come into a quiet haven.

Brasenose College, which is bounded on the east by Radcliffe Street and on the south by High Street, consists now of three quadrangles: namely, The Old Quadrangle, which is northernmost, and dates from 1509; the Middle Quadrangle, facetiously called "The Deer Park"; and the New Quadrangle (dating from 1887), which has a frontage to the High Street.

<small>94. Brasenose College.</small>

The Hall, which separates the two older quadrangles, is a noble room ornamented with a fine bay, stained glass window, a massive chimneypiece and portraits of founders and other notables connected with the college, including Robert Burton of *Anatomy of Melancholy* fame, and Dr. Nowel, Dean of St. Paul's, London—a good old man and "a dear lover and constant practiser of angling"; [1] while the famous Brazen Nose that gave the college its name hangs in a conspicuous place at the far end. The library, which dates from 1663, contains, besides much theological literature, a collection of Brasenose authors, a tenth century Terence, the manuscript of one of Bishop Pearson's works; and busts of Lord Grenville and Bishop Kaye. The Chapel, which is chiefly remarkable for its roof of elaborate fan tracery, has memorial windows to "Robertson of Brighton" [2] and the Rev. Dr. E. H. Cradock, who was Principal of Brasenose from 1853 to 1886, together with a tablet which it will be more appropriate to describe in our last chapter.

---

[1] *The Complete Angler* (Walton), Chapter I. Nowell died in 1601.

[2] Rev. F. W. Robertson died 15th August 1853.

REV. DR. HORNBY IN 1866.
Photo by Hills and Saunders, Oxford.

REV. CANON SHAND.
Photo by Hills and Saunders, Oxford.

Entering the great Quadrangle from Radcliffe Street, one is struck with the old-world beauty of the place, the architectural quaintnesses, the great chestnut that rises over its north walls, and the huge square blue sundial put there to tell of the march of time in a place where time never marches, and apparently never will march. **95. Pater's Rooms at Brasenose.** In the middle of the Quadrangle stood formerly a statuary group, which represented Samson braining a Philistine with the ass's jawbone,[1] said to have been—and Pater shared this erroneous opinion—a genuine work of the famous sculptor Giovanni of Bologna.[2]

Turning to our left we enter a doorway in the southeast corner of the Quadrangle; and, mounting a dark staircase (No. 7), presently find ourselves before Pater's rooms, which are two—a sitting-room or study, looking into Radcliffe Square, and a diminutive bedroom with a window in the corner of the old Quadrangle of Brasenose—perhaps the two most inconvenient rooms in the whole college. The sitting-room whose panelling, which extends from floor to ceiling, Pater coloured primrose, has two windows, and the one which projects, became, when furnished with cushioned seats, his favourite reading place. A square of tapestry, which he placed over the mantelpiece, and his carpet (a very handsome Persian, with yet many years of wear in it), still occupy their old places. His library, if so small a collection of books deserves so dignified a name, consisted of only as many volumes as were sufficient to fill a single low set of shelves. If he wanted a book he either went to the Bodleian or called on a friend; for he usually bought only cheap, paper-covered copies—with the result that almost the only really well-bound books in his possession were presentation volumes of poetry. "If it were practicable," he once said,[3] "I would read

[1] Sometimes wrongly called Cain and Abel.
[2] Jean Boullogne 1524—1608.
[3] To William Sharp about 1881. See *Atlantic Monthly*, December 1894.

all poetry for the first time in the handwriting of the poet. There is always, to me, an added charm when I can do so—an atmosphere. The poem gains, and my insight or sympathy is swifter and surer. I am conscious of this also in prose, though perhaps not so keenly, and certainly not so frequently. Of course there is one exception—every one, surely, must feel the same here; that is the instance of letters. Imagine the pleasure of reading the intimate letters of Michaelangelo, of Giorgione, of Leonardo, of Dante, of Spenser, of Shakespeare, of Goethe, in the originals! It would be like looking on a landscape of clear sunlight or moonlight, after having viewed it only through mist or haze."

Another "coquetry" of his room—to use his own expression—was a bust of Hercules (and we have already referred to the admiration displayed by the weakling Pater for men of muscle and sinew). "Hercules, Discobolus, Samson, these"—exclaimed one of Pater's admirers—"these be thy gods, O Pater." Beside an oval representing Venus, Cupid and the eagle of Jupiter in mid-air hung prints of "Paris awarding the apple" and "The Toilette of Venus." A Liberal in politics, he also placed on his walls a few pictures associated with the name of Liberty.[1] Join to this information the fact that he had for servant one Harry Charlwood—a good-looking man of middle-height, with dark whiskers and a fresh complexion—and one gets a very fair idea of Pater and his surroundings at the time he entered Brasenose.

Pater, as we said, had once more turned his attention to literature, but, so far as we are aware, he never again attempted verse. One day, he happened to be in the company of several friends who were discussing the immediate prospects of English poetry; and after listening to the

96. The Crystal Man.

---

[1] For description of Pater's rooms at a later day, see Chapter XL.

arguments for and against the various styles, he exclaimed, "You may be what you like, but as for me I have no ambition to shine except as a prose writer"— and with his glances directed towards the one large clear star of prose, and towards that only, he thenceforward pressed steadily on. Nothing, however, that he wrote during his early Brasenose period seems to have been preserved except an intensely interesting study entitled *Diaphanéité*. Students of Pater have been too busy fluttering round the *Renaissance* and *Marius* to pay much attention to this delightful morsel—which gives an insight into his life that can be obtained nowhere else. Besides, it is his first serious foray into a region of literature which he was to make peculiarly his own. It is his first Imaginary Portrait. *Diaphanéité*—or diaphaneity, to spell it the English way—is, of course, the quality of being diaphanous; and he imagined a man who should be as a crystal—who should be, furthermore, absolutely himself. Such a man might not be a man of culture, but he would be a man of taste, and Pater, who fondled the doctrine of the Pre-existence of Souls,[1] regarded taste, very beautifully, as "the reminiscence of a forgotten culture that once adorned the mind." This crystal man is uninfluenced by the times in which he lives. Raphael, in "the midst of the Reformation and the Renaissance, himself lighted up by them, yielded himself to neither." [2] Pater's own aim in life was to approach this type, and to a considerable extent he succeeded. Hitherto, he had been by turns, Keble, Kingsley, F. D. Maurice, A. P. Stanley, Heine, Voltaire, Goethe. Hitherto he had aped, not only in argument but also in tone of voice, the men who had for the moment fascinated him. Of all creatures he had been the most artificial, the most affected. He now

---

[1] See his remarks on *The Retreat* by Henry Vaughan, and Wordsworth's Ode on *The Intimations of Immortality*, *Plato and Platonism*, pp. 73 and 74.

[2] *Miscellaneous Studies*, p. 220.

grasped the fact that to produce our best we must be ourselves. An author who is indistinguishable from other people can never succeed either in stamping his own image on the minds of his contemporaries, or in fulfilling his mission. The one way to be entirely different from all other people is to be yourself; or to use Pater's words, "Simplicity in purpose and act is a kind of determinate expression in dexterous outline of one's personality." This intellectual type is not made up of several gifts which neutralize one another, it has one special gift which overtops all the others. Henceforth, we repeat, Walter Pater was to be Walter Pater, and as a result he stands quite apart from his contemporaries. He is isolated, and to use a favourite word of his own, columnar. The placid, white, marmoreal, monastic, subtle, equable, nebulous soul stands self-revealed. He is the nearest he could get to the Crystal Man.

There is one passage in *Diaphanéité* that might very well be omitted—that Pater himself, had he given it revision late in life, would certainly have omitted. However, the reader must treat this pretty sketch as he should treat all other literature; that is to say, gather to himself everything that is healthy and beautiful and ignore the rest. It has been stated [1] that in making the picture of the Crystal Man, Pater had in view the temperament of Mr. C. L. Shadwell, with whom he had recently formed a friendship. Whether that was so or not, it has been asserted by those who remember the Mr. Shadwell of those days that he was undoubtedly the handsomest man in the University—with a face like those to be seen on the finer Attic coins. But, as a matter of fact, it is far more probable that *Diaphanéité,* like all the rest of Pater's studies, is a compound—say of three men and a phantom.

[1] By Mr. A. C. Benson, for example.

BRASENOSE COLLEGE, OXFORD, SHOWING PATER'S ROOMS.
(ENTERED FROM THE DOORWAY IN THE CORNER.)

From a Photograph by Hills and Saunders, Oxford.

His year of probation having expired, Pater was on 5th February, 1865, elected Actual Fellow of Brazenose—the entry in the Vice-Principal's register running :

97. Actual Fellow of Brasenose, 5th Feb., 1865.

"February 5th (Sunday), 1865.

Mr. Principal [1]

Mr. V. P. (Menzies) [2]	Mr. Shand [5]
,, Turner [3]	,, Watson [6]
,, J. J. Hornby [4]	,, Yates [7]

Mr. John Davies Davenport, B.A., and Mr. Walter Horatio Pater, B.A., having completed their year of probation, were unanimously elected Actual Fellows."

Of the gentlemen mentioned in this paragraph, all of whom entered more or less into Pater's life, Mr. Principal (Rev. Dr. Cradock); Mr. Vice-Principal (Rev. Frederick Menzies, who became Canon of Christ Church); the Rev. Albert Watson,[8] who became Principal of Brasenose; and the Rev. William Yates, who became Rector of Cottingham, Uppingham, and Honorary Canon of Peterborough, are all dead. Mr. J. D. Davenport is now at the Chancery Bar, the Rev. Edward Tindal Turner still resides at Oxford, the Rev. Canon Thomas H. R. Shand, who left Oxford about 1869, is now Rector of Clayton, Sussex. The Rev. J. J. Hornby is now the Rev. Dr. Hornby and Provost of Eton. Asked for his recollections of Pater, Dr. Hornby laid most stress on Pater's "great attractiveness as a companion, his remarkable literary knowledge and

[1] Rev. Edward Hartopp Cradock.
[2] Rev. Frederick Menzies.
[3] Rev. Edward Tindal Turner.
[4] Rev. J. J. Hornby.
[5] Rev. Thomas H. R. Shand.
[6] Rev. Albert Watson.
[7] Rev. William Yates.
[8] He died in 1904.

insight, and the charm of his gentle, refined and simple character." "He was a very true and kind friend," continued Dr. Hornby, "but not very easy of access at the first, being rather shy and reticent towards those with whom he was not well acquainted. He was very kind and good to me, and always ready to impart his delightful criticisms and appreciations of art and literature, ancient and modern, which were so helpful and suggestive. I count it a great privilege to have known him even for the short time [1] that we were both resident together as Fellows of Brasenose." [2]

Of Dr. Cradock, the Principal, who had held his position since 1853, and was one of the most popular men in Oxford, it was said that even when his hair grew grey he was still but a youth, and his "sympathies were always with the young." There was no need at Brasenose, we are told, of "any tutor posing as the undergraduate's friend to stand between the wrath of Jove and the peccant mortal." The offenders knew that all due allowances would "be made for young blood and young heads on young shoulders." Brasenose was a great sporting college, and it was understood that the Doctor would not send down a man who was likely to do well on the river or in the cricket ground. Pater, on the other hand, took but a feeble interest in all these matters. His pulse, always a languid one—except when quickened by thoughts about art or literature—did not perceptibly increase its speed when he heard that the Brasenose boat rowed head of the river, or that Crowder and Crofts had "won the Pairs" and "Crofts the Sculls"; and he rarely mouthed the jargon of either the river or the football field. With his habit, however, of looking upon life with a half-amused expression, he enjoyed the absurdities of street, quad and lecture-room; and, fortunately, there was always some duffer to enliven

---

[1] Three years 1864—1867.

[2] Letter to me 8th December 1905.

BRASENOSE COLLEGE FROM RADCLIFFE SQUARE.

SHOWING THE LIBRARY (THE BUILDING ON THE LEFT) AND PATER'S WINDOWS TO THE RIGHT OF THE LIBRARY DOOR, AND ON THE SECOND STOREY.

Photo by Hills and Saunders.

the general somnolence of the place. Among the features of Brasenose, for example, were Mr. Yates's Sunday afternoon lectures on the Greek Testament, and one of the men on being called upon to translate

οὐχ οὗτός ἐστιν ὁ τοῦ τέκτονος υἱός; [1]

exclaimed triumphantly: "This man is not the son of his father"—a rendering which, thanks to the charm of its originality, made the round of the college.

From the study of Goethe it was but a step to the Renaissance, and Pater now gave all his attention to the great intellectual movement which vivified Europe between the thirteenth and the seventeenth centuries; and with his passion for it there grew up in him an ardent desire to visit its principal home; consequently, in 1865, he and Mr. C. Lawrence Shadwell set out for Italy, and visited, among other towns, Ravenna, Pisa and Florence. The scenery naturally enchanted him—the brown windy turrets, "the straw-coloured fields," "the forest arabesques," the "cool colour and tranquillising line of the distant Alps, the poplar-fringed watercourses"—but—loving men rather than meadows—his chief delight was to recall, amid their haunts, the master minds of the Renaissance, and to draw mental pictures of them.

98. In Italy with Mr. C. L. Shadwell, 1865.

Together with his study of the Renaissance, Pater was giving his mind to some of the leading authors in English literature, and particularly to Coleridge, Lamb and Sir Thomas Browne. He commences the first of these studies —an article in *The Westminster Review* on Coleridge—by pointing out that Modern thought is distinguished from Ancient thought by its cultivation of Relativity instead of Absolutism. Ancient Philosophy tried to classify everything—to put a ring fence round

99. The Influence of Coleridge, Jan., 1866.

---

[1] St. Matthew, XIII., 55.

things; the modern spirit holds that nothing can be rightly known except relatively and under conditions. "The literary life of Coleridge," observes Pater, "was a disinterested struggle against the relative spirit." He tries to fix scientific truth in absolute formulas. He regarded the then recent metaphysics of Germany—born of Kant and Schelling—as a legitimate expansion of the teaching of Plato, and spent all his life in endeavouring to present them to English readers. This was "the one thread of continuity in a life otherwise singularly wanting in unity of purpose," and to impress the fact upon the reader is the principal aim of Pater's article. Even the remarks on Coleridge's marvellous poetry, and the citations from it, have in view the same object.

Speaking of this article (which, by-the-by, has pleased nobody), and the article on Rossetti, Mr. Watts-Dunton, in conversation with the present writer, once described them as the two worst essays on those subjects he had ever read, and then he dwelt on the inequality of Pater, who, along with the finest work, wrote so much that is scarcely third-rate.

One result of the study of Coleridge and Coleridge's life was to implant in Pater the desire to become a Unitarian minister; but, after nursing the idea several months, he abandoned it for ever.

PATER'S SITTING-ROOM AT BRASENOSE.
Photo by W. H. Payne, St. Aldate's, Oxford.

2, BRADMORE ROAD, NORHAM GARDENS, OXFORD.
PATER TOOK THIS HOUSE IN 1869, AND GAVE IT UP IN 1886.

Photo by Hills and Saunders, Oxford.

CHAPTER XXVII

FEBRUARY 1866—13TH NOVEMBER 1870

ART FOR ART'S SAKE

BIBLIOGRAPHY :

19. Winckelmann. *Westminster Review*, January 1867.
20. Æsthetic Poetry. Written in 1868.
21. Notes on Leonardo da Vinci. *Fortnightly Review*, November 1869.
22. Sandro Botticelli. *Fortnightly Review*, August 1870.

We now approach the period when Pater began to write his remarkable work on the Renaissance, the kernel of which is the presentation of the theory that art should be pursued for its own sake. Most writers who have attempted to deal with the origin and scope of this work have made the most curious blunders. Some of them were evidently under the delusion that the phrase *Art for Art's sake* was originated by Pater—that he was the first upon whom the idea dawned—a delusion ridiculous enough, seeing that years and years before Pater's time artists and writers had formed themselves into two camps—the Classic, who held that every work of art should have a moral, and the Romantic, whose blazon was *L'art pour l'art*.

100. Art for Art's Sake.

"*L'art pour l'art*," says Théophile Gautier, the greatest and doughtiest of all the devotees and defenders of the formula, "signifies for the artist a method of working disengaged from all preoccupation save of that which in itself is beautiful. In the light of this doctrine, when rightly understood, all subjects are indifferent and acquire value only in proportion to the sentiment, style and power of ideal presentment brought to bear on them by the individual artist. . . . When Shakespeare wrote *Othello* he had no other object than to show a man under the influence of jealousy; Voltaire, on the contrary, in composing his tragedy of *Mahomet,* proposed not only to represent the figure of the prophet, but to demonstrate generally the effects of fanaticism, and by inference, in particular, the vices of the Catholic and other Christian orders of his day. The consequence is that his tragedy suffers from the introduction of a heterogeneous element, and in endeavouring to compass a philosophic effect, he fails to attain the æsthetic perfection of the thing absolutely beautiful—whilst *Othello,* on the contrary, although without pretension to undermine the most insignificant superstition or to remove the smallest prejudice, reaches heights of sublimity and beauty that are far beyond the attainment of *Mahomet,* despite the encyclopædical tirades of which the latter is full. . . . . The programme of the modern school is to seek out beauty for itself with a complete impartiality, a perfect disinterestedness, without counting for success upon allusions or tendencies foreign to the subject under treatment; and I believe that this is assuredly the most philosophic manner of considering art." [1]

Among those who assimilated this theory was Mr. A. C. Swinburne, with whose fame all England was then ringing—men being unable to praise sufficiently the beauty, the subtle artistry and the music of those wonderful poems, "Itylus," "Hesperia," "The Garden of Proserpine," and their companions. Stricken, as were so many others with what has been called "The Swinburnian Fever," Pater sought the company of Mr. Swinburne, but his acquaintance with the poet was very slight; and presently we find him a member of that brilliant circle of poets and artists—chiefly young men—of whom "Art

101. The Swinburnian Fever.

[1] Theophile Gautier, *Du Beau dans l'Art* (1856). Translated by Mr. John Payne in his essay on *The Poets of the Neo-Romantic School in France.*

for Art's Sake" was the watchword—a circle [1] which included John Payne, Arthur O'Shaughnessy,[2] J. T. Nettleship, and Simeon Solomon [3]—the studios of the two last being some of their meetings places.

Speaking of what he calls "the favourite contention of the Classic School that an art work should be judged by its usefulness, or, to use a more comprehensive word, its truth," Mr. John Payne says [4] "Those who seek for truth in art, as the end, follow a delusive aim, that can but result in the enfeebling of their own powers and landing them in the sandy deserts of didacticism. They forget that beauty is necessarily truth; indeed, it is, in the words of the divine pupil of Socrates, the splendour of truth—that is to say, something higher and more noble than truth itself. Truth, on the contrary, is not necessarily beautiful; and as art without beauty cannot exist, truth *per se* can never be its object."

Of Mr. Payne's poems, the passionate "Rime of Redemption," the musical "Songs of Life and Death," etc., of O'Shaughnessy's volumes *An Epic of Women, Lays of France, Music and Moonlight* and *Songs of a Worker,* of the earlier (mystic) drawings of Nettleship, and of the paintings of Simeon Solomon, we need only say that all of them were inspired by the dictum "Art for Art's Sake;" [5] and that the phrase was constantly

---

[1] Some of the members of this circle Pater scarcely knew at all. With others he was extremely intimate.

[2] O'Shaughnessy, who was in the Natural History Department of the British Museum, died 31st January, 1881, aged 36.

[3] A man of real genius, Solomon had no persistent energy and no tenacity of purpose. His favourite scheme was to paint a picture of Melchizedek, which would doubtless have been a masterpiece. He was also an author, and in 1871 published a curious work entitled: *A Vision of Love Revealed in Sleep,* in which he attempted to explain the mysticism of his paintings. See *The Cam,* 14th February, 1906. Article by Mr. Oscar Browning.

[4] In his article "The Poet."

[5] In his sparkling volume of essays, *Without Prejudice* (1896), Mr. Israel Zangwill advances the theory that with Pater the formula of "Art for Art's Sake" was for the *spectator* of art, not for the *maker of art.* In the light of history, however, this theory entirely breaks down.

in the mouths of the members of the circle years before Pater had ever even heard of it.

Up to this period Pater had drawn inspiration chiefly from Ruskin, whom he found too chilly, and Goethe, whom he thought "constrained." He himself, all on fire for beauty that enthralled—that ensorcelled the senses—and with his natural heat raised by contact with the English Romanticists, had arrived at a state of mind which can be best compared to that in which Keats found himself when planning *Endymion*—the whirl which made possible the outburst commencing "A thing of beauty is a joy for ever;" and, like Keats, Pater was to elevate the pursuit of beauty to the rank of a religion. It was while he was in this state of tension that there came under his notice the newly-published Biographical Essays of Otto Jahn,[1] one of which, *The Life of Winckelmann*,[2] absorbed him as he had been absorbed by no other writing. In Winckelmann he saw his own identical self—an impassioned, flashing soul who flung off without hesitation anything and everything that seemed likely to interfere with his one great aim in life —"to attain the knowledge of beauty." Employed in the day time as a teacher, Winckelmann robs himself of sleep in order to gain time for reading. He finds that the study of mathematics and law made it impossible for him to devote himself as he wished to the arts. Out of the window go his mathematical and law books. His religion—Lutheranism—turns out to be a bar to studying art at Rome. Out of the window goes his religion too—or rather the shreds of it that were left after the

[margin: 102. Winckelmann, Jan. 1867. Oscar Browning.]

---

[1] Otto Jahn, archæologist (1813—1869). His *Biographische Aufsätze* appeared in 1866.

[2] Johann Joachim Winckelmann, critic and historian of Greek art. Born at Stendal in Prussian Saxony in 1717. Studied at Dresden. Turned Roman Catholic on being promised an appointment at Rome, where he studied antiquities and wrote his principal works. In 1768 when returning to Rome after a visit to Vienna, he was murdered in a hotel at Trieste by a fellow-traveller to whom he had shown some gold coins.

sympathetic study of the works of Voltaire; and he becomes, nominally, at any rate, a devout son of the Roman Church. Walter Pater, reading this, seemed to see a reflection of his own self. Had not he, too, flung aside unhesitatingly both friends and religion because they seemed clogs to his progress towards the shrine of Truth in the Temple of Beauty! And this is how he excuses both Winckelmann and himself. "To that transparent nature, with its simplicity as of the earlier world, the loss of absolute sincerity must have been a real loss . . . . yet at the bar of the highest criticism, perhaps, Winckelmann may be absolved. The sincerity of his religious profession was only one incident of a culture in which the moral instinct, like the religious or political, was merged in the artistic." [1]

Pater is generally held to have been of a sluggish, cold nature, and, admittedly, there was a passivity, an unbroken calm about his latter days; but in this early period, as we have shown, he was, when provoked by art and literature, all fire, and it was, certainly, to use his own words, the "enthusiasm" burning "like lava," and "the feverish nursing of the one motive of his life," that attracted him so much in Winckelmann's character. It is, however, in the concluding sentence of his essay that Pater reveals himself most distinctly. He had been speaking of the toilsome life of certain groups of men and women, embarrassed by the great laws of nature, but who yet work out for themselves a supreme *dénouement*. "Who," cries Pater, in white heat, "who, if he saw through all, would fret against the chain of circumstance which endows one at the end with those great experiences?" Pater himself, indeed, burnt ardently to do notable work in the world and to win the plaudits of the finest minds. He was struggling onward, upwards, often disheartened, in that city of virgin ice—discouraging, depressing Oxford—in which to exhibit a spark of enthusiasm for any mortal thing under the

[1] *Renaissance*, p. 185.

sun is to stamp yourself as a freak of nature, and to attract glances of astonishment, not unmingled with pity; and it is a noteworthy fact that to Oxford, Pater, as a man of genius, owed absolutely nothing. All his inspiration came from elsewhere. Yet, notwithstanding his rebuffs, he recognises that all is for the best—that the very difficulties he encounters are putting grit into him, and he can patiently await the *dénouement*. Come what would, he was resolved to live intensely "in his best self and in the highest moments of his best self," by detaching from his intellectual force, as he says in 'Winckelmann,' "all flaccid interests." Life, he recognises, is slipping away. "Well," he observes, "we cannot alter the fact. If all is passing away, let the knowledge of this be a stimulus towards intenser activity, let it excite within us the thirst for a full and perfect experience." On the brilliance and suggestiveness of this essay—which reminds the reader of nothing so much as the flash of sabres, it is unnecessary to dwell. The eaglet had found its wings, and its flight henceforward was to be proud and triumphant.

The essay on Winckelmann had the effect of securing for Pater at least one new friend, namely Mr. Oscar Browning, who met him, shortly after, at the breakfast-table of a common acquaintance—Mr. Joseph Payne. Pater's appearance, says Mr. Browning, was "heavy and uncomely," "but this outside concealed a soul of rare and precious quality. He seemed to me to go about the world with a Diogenes lantern, seeking for beauty everywhere and finding it in the most unlikely places."

As a tutor Pater was scarcely a success, being, as we have already observed, no scholar, as Oxford understands the word. His weakness in Latin and Greek, for example, was perfectly well known not only among the dons of Brasenose and other colleges, but also to his own pupils. "In my first term," writes the Rev. Anthony Bathe to the author, "it was the business of Pater, as tutor, to give

103. Pater no Scholar.

MR. RICHARD ROBINSON.

Photo by Hills and Saunders, Oxford.

REV. A. J. DODGSON.
[LEWIS CARROLL.]

Photo by Hills and Saunders, Oxford.

WALTER PATER.

FROM AN OIL PAINTING BY MR. W. S. WRIGHT.

This portrait is founded on several early portraits.

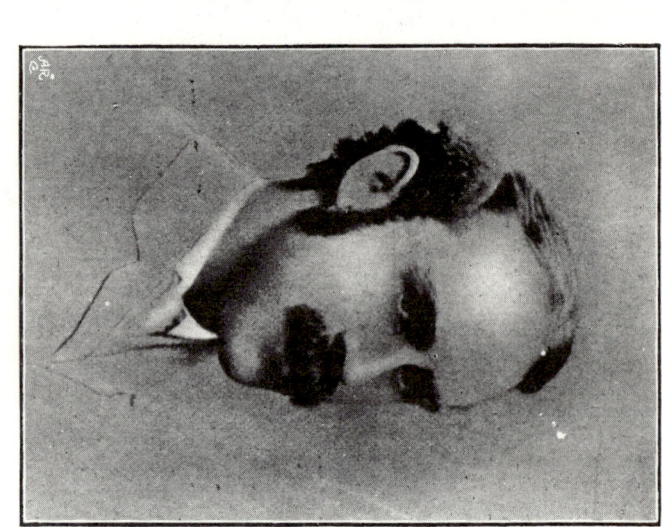

WALTER PATER.

FROM A GROUP TAKEN AT BRASENOSE.

Kindly lent by Rev. A. J. Galpin, M.A., Headmaster of the King's School, Canterbury.

us freshmen lectures in the *Georgics;* and he was much at sea in them. On one occasion he insisted in translating *fragili.* .... *stringeret hordea culmo* (*Georgics* i., 317), 'fills the barns with grain,' instead of 'binds the sheaves with the brittle straw.' (1) He persisted in his translation, and of course we gave way, but I suppose he saw that something was wrong, for after this we had to write out the construe, and our exercises were not returned to us."

It was at this time one of the duties of the tutors of Brasenose to give Divinity Lectures to their pupils. Very often Pater shirked them; but his pupils, having discovered that he disliked the task and would gladly have had no class, took particular pains to be present and punctual. Finally he seized the bull by the horns, and boldly discontinued them. The Rev. Oswald Birchall, who was at Brasenose from 1864 to 1867, says, "I attended Pater's lectures on Aristotle. He was distinguished from the Positivist teachers of those days by his ability to understand the point of view and the thoughts of the people from whom he differed. His way was not so much to search out the meaning of Aristotle or to help scholars to understand him, as to take a text and pour out, extempore, the thoughts which it suggested to himself—comparing or contrasting Aristotle with other philosophers. His manner in lecturing was to bend his head over the table at which he sat, and cover his eyes with his hands, not often looking up to ask a question." (2)

Another of Pater's pupils was John Wordsworth (3) grandson of the poet's brother Christopher—whose name alone would have given him favour in Pater's eyes. Tutor and pupil became fast friends, and on one occasion Wordsworth was a member of a reading party

---

(1) This passage may also be rendered "Strips the barley[s] of the fragile haulm." Hordea (plural), peculiar to Virgil for hordeum.

(2) Letters of Rev. Oswald Birchall to me, June 1904.

(3) Deacon 1867, priest 1869, Fellow of Brasenose 1866—1871.

who accompanied Pater into Wales. In 1867 Wordsworth became a Fellow of Brasenose, and his subsequent brilliant career, which culminated in his elevation to the episcopate, is well known. At the end of 1869 Pater and his sisters took a house in Norham Gardens, No. 2, Bradmore Road, where he was visited by Mr. John Morley, the Rev. M. B. Moorhouse, Mr. Francis Percival, the Rev. O. G. Sidgwick, and other friends; and he not infrequently met Miss Jean Ingelow, the poetess.

His principal friends, however, were the Rev. C. L. Dodgson and Mr. Richard Robinson. Charles Lutwidge Dodgson, who was a student of Christ Church, had from 1855 been mathematical lecturer there. In 1865, under the name of Lewis Carroll, he issued *Alice in Wonderland*, now a nursery classic, and in 1867 he went on a tour in Russia with Liddon.[1] The one attraction Pater found in Dodgson was his humour, and the friends spent many a merry hour together in Dodgson's rooms at Christ Church. But Pater found the learning of Richard Robinson an even more powerful loadstone. Since 1865, when he had become a fellow of Queen's, Robinson had devoted himself almost wholly to historical and legal study, going by preference into obscure and outlying regions where access was difficult. On two subjects—the history of the English Universities and the history of the Commonwealth—he had amassed an unrivalled store of learning. Indeed, of the pamphlet literature of the 17th and 18th centuries no man could possibly have had a more extensive knowledge.[2] He had ranged "From Ursa Major to the Blackmoor's Spall."[3] His attitude towards religion was that of "a somewhat aggressive Agnostic." "All the same," writes a gentleman who knew him intimately, "I

104. Rev. C. L. Dodgson and Richard Robinson.

---

[1] See *Life and Letters of Henry Parry Liddon*, p. 100.
[2] See *The Academy* 1870, article by Professor Sayce.
[3] Du Bellay, translated by John Payne.

remember his saying in a lecture that 'viewed from the outside one is forced to conclude that man is subject to Necessity, but viewed from the inside one is forced to believe that he has Freewill.' [1] I have never seen the case stated in the same way elsewhere. To me, after years of reflection, it appears to sum up the whole position." Another who knew him—the Rev. Oswald Birchall—says, "He was an incessant talker, both in public and in private; in public about Liberalism, and in private about the miscellaneous books which he had been reading. Besides being a student, he found time to help and encourage the younger men about him, and when in London took a night class of youths in the East End." For no man in Oxford, indeed, had a more brilliant career been predicted. Yet his extraordinary knowledge was to be comparatively resultless. In the beginning of November, 1870, he was strong and well; a fortnight later he lay in his coffin. Beyond a few articles contributed to magazines and newspapers [2] and half-a-dozen papers read before learned societies, he had been able to do nothing. Still his life was not without fruit. Two men in particular were never weary of proclaiming their indebtedness to him and the stimulus received from his amazing individuality—namely, A. H. Sayce [3] and Walter Pater.

Richard Robinson was carried to Littlemore Churchyard—many mourning-coaches and private carriages

---

[1] This observation is adapted from Schopenhauer.

[2] 1867—The University of Oxford from 1650 to 1750, *Oxford Undergraduates' Journal*. 1868—January, Commemoration during the last century, *Macmillan's Magazine*. 1868—October, The Nonconformist at Oxford, *Theological Review*. 1869—September, Anecdotes of the London Poor, *Macmillan's Magazine*. This year he lectured on "The Two Sieges of Bristol" and "The English Revolution." In *The Academy* (Vols. I. and II.) he wrote reviews of Nehemiah Wallington's *Historical Notices of Events chiefly in the Reign of Charles I.* (Vol. I., p. 186); Baker's *History of St. John's College, Cambridge* (Vol. I., p. 219); Clement Markham's *The Great Lord Fairfax* (Vol. II., p. 18); Spedding's *Life and Letters of Bacon* (Vol. II.).

[3] I am indebted to Professor Sayce for these particulars.

and all the undergraduates of Queen's College following the hearse. The cross on his grave has the wording:

In Memory of
RICHARD ROBINSON, M.A.,
Fellow, Tutor, and Librarian
of Queen's College, Oxford,
And Student of the Inner Temple.
Born May 23, 1844.
Died November 13, 1870.

And on the west side of the church is a tablet with an inscription in Latin, written, we believe, by Mr. Humphry Ward.

HIC JACET
INGENII. LABORIS. MODESTIAE. SPECIMEN
R.R
QVEM SVBITO ABREPTVM
LVGENT AMICI, DESIDERAT ACADEMIA
REQVIRIT PATRIA.

"What knowledge," remarked Mark Pattison to Professor Sayce, "has perished with him! How vain seems all toil to acquire." [1]

---

[1] Mrs. Humphry Ward has an allusion to the death of Robinson in *Robert Elsmere*, and quotes Pattison's remark. (Chapter XLI.)

CHAPTER XXVIII

13TH NOVEMBER 1870—DECEMBER 1873

THE RENAISSANCE

BIBLIOGRAPHY:

23. Pico della Mirandola. *Fortnightly Review*, October 1871.
24. Poetry of Michaelangelo. *Fortnightly Review*, November 1871.
25. Studies in the History of the Renaissance. February 1873.

Several other articles had by this time left Pater's pen—those on Leonardo, Botticelli, Pico and Michaelangelo having been sent to the *Fortnightly Review*, which was then under the editorship of Mr. John Morley. After thoroughly revising them, Pater added to them his article on Winckelmann and some other studies, and issued the whole in book form with the title *The Renaissance: Studies in Art and Poetry*, which he dedicated to his friend, C. L. Shadwell. Without doubt, *The Renaissance* is Pater's masterpiece. Few more stimulating works have left the Press; no man can read it without being thrilled—raised above himself—excited to more strenuous effort. Very slowly had this rampired city risen, but its foundation is laid with sapphires and all its borders are pleasant stones. *Marius* and everything else that he did pale before the barbaric beauty of this gorgeous structure.

Pater's teaching is briefly this: "Imitate the men of the Renaissance and enjoy yourself." Like them, you will find your keenest delight in the "attitude of the scholar," in "the enthusiastic acquisition of knowledge

105. Humanism.

for its own sake."⁽¹⁾ Among the features of that great period was a revival of interest in the classics and in Greek sculpture. Homer, Æschylus, Ovid, Virgil, Horace, who had so long lain dank or dusty and forgotten in ancient libraries, were taken down, dried or cleansed and studied with enthusiasm, and the poetical idea found acceptance that the old deities, supposed to be dead, had begun to quit their hiding-places—an idea which Heine *(Gods in Exile)* and Pater who followed him, play with again and again.⁽²⁾

Those who harked back to the classics and the ideas of the Pagan World gave themselves the name of humanists ⁽³⁾—and the intensity of their worship of beauty led them to place it higher even than the Christian ideal. "The essence of humanism," says Pater, "is that belief that nothing which has ever interested living men and women can lose its vitality— no language they have spoken, nor oracle beside which they have hushed their voices, no dream which has once been entertained by actual human minds, nothing about which they have ever been passionate, or expended time and zeal." ⁽⁴⁾ A latter-day humanism had, indeed, by this time become Pater's creed. Faun, Christian knight, satyr, martyr, Mary the Virgin, and Venus, who, apparently, was not a virgin, ægipan and Pantheist, all hob-nobbed together amicably in his tolerant brain ; and his conversation comported with his writings. In one breath he would make utterances that befitted a Voltaire, and in the next express the hope that he would be buried in the robes of a Capuchin. Although, however, Pater's Humanism is conspicuous enough in his

⁽¹⁾ *Miscellaneous Studies* (Raphael), p. 26.
⁽²⁾ See *Renaissance*, pp. 24, 32, 118. *Miscellaneous Studies:* Apollo in Picardy; Raphael. *Imaginary Portraits:* Denys l'Auxerrois.
⁽³⁾ Latin, Litteræ Humaniores : polite letters.
⁽⁴⁾ *Renaissance*, p. 49.

Renaissance, that book in reality neither gains nor loses by it—the qualities that have immortalised it being quite independent of the creed of the writer.

Let us now examine briefly this seductive book—commencing with the Preface, which is one of its most inspiring portions. Our business, says Pater, is to know one's own impression of an object. We are to ask ourselves, "What is this song or picture, this engaging personality presented in life or in a book to *me?* What effect does it really produce on me?" The function of the æsthetic critic is, he says, to indicate the special virtue or property in an object of beauty that causes the pleasurable impression. All which remarks are none the less valuable because they are not original, being lifted almost bodily, and without acknowledgment from Goethe's *Autobiography.*[1] As an example of a writer who gives intense pleasure Pater takes Wordsworth, and lays down that the great charm in him is his habit of imparting life and feeling, as it were, to objects of nature. There, then, says Pater, you have the *virtue,* the active principle in Wordsworth's poems.

106. Burn with a Gem-like Flame.

The opening essay in the book is an attempt to prove that there was a literary and artistic revival before the Renaissance period—a sort of false dawn; and he tells the stories of *Amis and Amile* and *Aucassin and Nicolette,"* both of which, he insists, reveal a yearning after freedom and beauty and a revolt against the faith of the times. The old gods, shaking off their disguises are already beginning to peep from their hiding-places. Venus, tired of her caves [2] and bats, had already yoked

---

[1] Goethe's words are: "It is everybody's duty to seek out for what is internal and peculiar in a book which particularly interests him, and at the same time, above all things, to weigh in what relation it stands to his own inner nature, and how far, by that vitality, his own is excited and rendered faithful." Bk. 12.

[2] Tannhäuser in the German legend comes to the Venusberg [perhaps the Horselberg, near Eisenach], and enters a cave palace where he beholds the wonders of Venus and her court. Upon this legend is founded Mr. Swinburne's splendid poem, "Laus Veneris," Def. Ed. i., p. 11.

her car with sparrows; Apollo, having snapped in twain his shepherd's crook, was furbishing up his rusty lyre; the aged Jupiter, who, clad in rabbit skins [1]—a sort of polar Robinson Crusoe—had for five hundred years pottered about the icebergs of Spitzbergen, was moving southward. In short, Olympus was once more beginning to get saucy. Heine, shaking his ribald sides, could enter into the humour of it all, but Pater is as sober as a Georgian Quaker. Each, however, has his special charm, and we shall presently see Pater, in his own peculiar and delicate way, elaborating these ideas—making Bacchus return to sunlight in the guise of Denys l'Auxerrois, and presenting to us an Apollo redivivus—namely, Brother Apollyon—who kills over again his darling Hyacinthus.

The essay on the versatile Florentine Pico della Mirandola is followed by that on Botticelli, the painter whose Madonnas, were, to Pater's seeming, all but infidels "shrinking from the pressure of the divine child," and pleading "in unmistakable undertones for a warmer, lower humanity"—those peevish-looking Madonnas who are neither for "Jehovah nor for his enemies." It was Botticelli, it will be remembered, who was charged with the heresy [2] of assuming that the human race are an incarnation of those angels who in the great revolt of Lucifer remained neutral; and Pater, who pleases himself with the assumption that the charge was true, ranks Botticelli among those who take no side in great conflicts. "He thus sets for himself the limits within which art, undisturbed by any moral ambition, does its most sincere and surest work." The chapter on "The Poetry of Michaelangelo" is chiefly attractive by reason of the remarks on clairvoyance—a subject, however, which is dealt with at much greater length in the finest essay in the book—that on Leonardo da Vinci,

---

[1] See Heine's *Gods in Exile*.

[2] His "heretic picture" in the National Gallery will be remembered.

Pater makes out Leonardo to have been a prince of clairvoyants in an age of clairvoyance and divination. His women "are the clairvoyants, through whom, as through delicate instruments, one becomes aware of the subtler forces of nature." Whether these ideas are tenable or not we need not trouble to ask. It is sufficient to know that this was the impression that Leonardo's paintings had on the poetic eye of Pater; and then the article blossoms into that perfect flower—the description of Monna Lisa—the presence that "rose so strangely beside the waters," and that seemed to Pater "expressive of what in the ways of a thousand years men had come to desire." He had, indeed, looked into that face until it fashioned itself into an elaborate poem. The essay on the School of Giorgione abounds in fine passages, but the most rememberable is that in which Pater inculcates the importance of attending to the little things of life—"gestures and speech and the details of daily intercourse." True enough, a simple inclination of the head may robe a wilderness with blossoms. Beatrice made to Dante a "most sweet salutation"; and all thoughtful men to all time will benefit.

Coming to Joachim du Bellay—a selection of whose principal lyrical poems, by-the-by, will shortly be presented to the British public by Mr. John Payne in his forthcoming *Flowers of France*,[1]—Pater, following Sainte-Beuve, finds that the virtue or active principle in

[1] *Flowers of France*: representative French poems from the beginning to the present day, rendered into English verse in accordance with the original forms by John Payne. The first section (Vols. IV. and V.), dealing with the Romantic Period (Victor Hugo to Leconte de Lisle) of the Nineteenth Century has recently been issued by the Villon Society (Hon. Sec., Mr. Alfred Forman, 49, Comeragh Road, West Kensington); and another section, Vol. II., dealing with the Renaissance Period (Ronsard to Saint-Amant) of the Sixteenth Century, is now in the press, and will follow shortly. Three other sections, *i.e.*, Vol. I., The Dawn (Thirteenth, Fourteenth and Fifteenth Centuries), Vol. III., The Dark Ages (Seventeenth and Eighteenth Centuries), and Vol. VI., The Decadence (Present Time), will complete the work, which will thus present a complete Florilegium of French poetry, whilst each section forms an independent work, complete in itself.

him is his proclivity to portray his "own most intimate moods and to take the reader into his confidence"—a characterisation which, seeing that it is common to most lyrical poets, cannot be said to have much depth. There is one quality in Du Bellay which is far more prominent than his intimacy, and that is the perpetual sadness of the man who spent the best years of his life in what was to him an abhorrent exile at Rome. But Pater's article gives an entirely erroneous impression of its subject, for we might judge from it that Du Bellay's verses (and he calls Du Bellay "almost the poet of one poem") are really little more than mere thistledown—light, pretty, silvery things that blow about. "The Winnower's Song," however, is not at all representative of Du Bellay in general—the bulk of that writer's work being, as will be seen from the following fair specimen of it —a sonnet—which Mr. John Payne allows us to print— of a much more substantial nature:

TO A DEAD FRIEND.
At last, after long years of wandering on the strand,
Where we the sorry sort of courtiers see complain,
The goal all seek it hath been given thee to attain,
From poortith's tristful thrall delivered and unbanned.
We others, left behind on shore, meanwhile, from land
Unto the boatmen deaf our arms stretch out in vain,
Who chases us afar; for nought but a quatrain,
The ferryage to pay, alack! we have in hand.
So, where, among the shades, the dwellings of the blest,
The lovers of old time enjoy the eternal rest,
Thou with try lady walk'st, like them, the Elysian shore;
Oblivion's long-drawn draught thou drink'st of travails past,
Heedless of those whom thou hast in Life's chains left fast,
Yet bawling on the quays and tugging at the oar.

Pater's remarks on Du Bellay, indeed, would have been applied more felicitously to another member of the Pleiad,[1] Remy Belleau—the sweetest and daintiest of the seven.

Of the next essay—that on Winckelmann—we have already spoken; and, lastly, there is the famous "Conclusion," with its admonition that we should make it the business of our life to endeavour to be present

[1] The members of the Pleiad were Jean Dorat, Pontus de Tyard, Pierre de Ronsard, Joachim du Bellay, J. A. Baïf, Remy Belleau and Etienne Jodelle.

always "at the focus where the greatest number of vital forces unite in their purest energy. To burn always with this hard gem-like flame, to maintain this ecstasy, is success in life. Our lives are brief—our one chance of lengthening them is to get 'as many pulsations as possible into the given time.'" [1] This can best be accomplished, we are assured, by feeding the passion for art and poesy—"for art comes to you professing frankly to give nothing but the highest quality to your moments as they pass, and simply for those moments' sake."

And so finishes what men in their admiration for it have described as "the Golden Book"—a title which, in a sense, it deserves. Indeed, to read only the "Conclusion" is to feel one's heart moved more than with a trumpet. That the book has its blemishes—and grave blemishes —we are by no means the first to notice. Amid the rose and the lily and the fruit trees with propped branches one detects here and there the nightshade and the mad-apple. To use some favourite words of Pater's —perhaps written by Pater—

Weedes ne doubt there be,
The which yourselves must delve and grubbe up carefullie. [2]

But the virtues of the book are so conspicuous that these weeds do not seriously interfere with it.

The *Renaissance* had a mixed reception. Some readers—nay many—were provoked by it; some had eyes only for the "weedes"; others were carried off their feet by the more dazzling passages—as, for example, that about the "gem-like flame." Nobody accepts everything that Pater chooses to enounce. The theory that art should be followed for art's sake will, we suppose, to all time set son against father, father against son. Some will smile at the idea of Leonardo's women being clairvoyants; others will agree with the *Blackwood's* critic who stigmatised the theory respecting Botticelli's Madonnas as "one of the most incon-

[1] See also *Marius*, Vol. I., p. 144.
[2] See first page of Vol. I.

gruous and grotesque misrepresentations ever invented by man." But accept what you like, reject what you like—the fundamental greatness of the book remains. Of Pater's style we shall speak later.

The Rector of Lincoln College, which adjoins Brasenose, was in those days the bibliomaniacal and scholarly Mark Pattison, who, to use the words of M. Taine, written after a visit to Oxford in 1871, resided in "the prettiest nest you could imagine of crumbling architecture, ivy and noble trees"—the "Rector's Lodge." And if Taine was drawn to Pattison he was even more closely drawn to the *"jolie jeune* Mme. Pattison," whom he described as twenty-six, though she was really a little older, and as being, not only the leading mind of Oxford feminine society in the domain of literature and art, but also "an erudite authority on everything pertaining to the French Renaissance."[1] With his intense love for books, Pattison was apt to speak of them in the terms usually employed towards beloved children. He crooned, indeed, over a favourite as a mother does over an infant. He could never work away from his books. The poet Schiller, it seems, always kept rotten apples in his study—imagining that their scent was beneficial to him. Pointing to the shelves that supported his treasures, Pattison used to say: "There are my rotten apples." Whether at Lincoln College or at 2, Bradmore Road, Pater and Pattison often chatted together about books, though sometimes Pattison, in his perversity, would taboo the subject. At one of these meetings at Bradmore Road (Mr. Edmund Gosse,[2] who had recently made Pater's acquaintance, being present), Pattison talked fascinatingly and illuminatingly; and on leaving asked Pater and Mr. Gosse to pay him a visit at Lincoln next day. They accordingly

107. Mr. and Mrs. Mark Pattison.

[1] In his *Renaissance* Pater refers to Mrs. Mark Pattison's book, *The Renaissance of Art in France*, as "a work of great taste and learning."
[2] See *Critical Kit-Kats*.

went, but the charm was broken, Pattison talked "of nothing but croquet and petticoats," and on leaving the college Pater expressed his belief that Pattison liked nothing better than "romping with great girls round gooseberry bushes." If, however, Pattison loved a little nonsense, Pater was not averse from it either. As we have already several times observed, he was an incorrigible mimic, and there was not a single personage in the circle of his friends whom he did not at one time or another take off. He liked to imagine Pattison as disturbed at midnight by a burglar.[1] The Rector leaping from bed is confronted with a dark lantern and a revolver. "If it's books you want,'' cries the Rector—and Pater imitated Pattison's querulous voice—"I am in your hands. Make a selection, but be merciful. But if you want silver, you'd better go over to ——'s [and Pater varied the name according to taste]. I'm a poor man and have nothing but plated goods, but —— is rich and has the real thing. A smug fellow is ——."

No one read Pater's *Renaissance* more eagerly than Mrs. Mark Pattison, and though she handled it with some severity in her survey of it in the *Westminster Review* she paid an ungrudging tribute to its unique and grateful bouquet. Curious to say, she was the one critic who ever stumbled upon the precise truth about Pater. She declared that Pater was lacking both in knowledge of the times of which the art of the Renaissance was an outcome, and in scientific method. He wrote of the Renaissance, she said, as if it was an "air-plant independent of the ordinary sources of nourishment . . . a sentimental revolution having no relation to the conditions of the actual world. . . We miss the sense of the connection between art and literature and the other forms of life of which they are the outward expression, and feel as if we were wandering in a world of unsubstantial dreams." But while denying the writer's intimate possession of his subject,

---

[1] There are several variants of this tale.

she admitted, as we have already observed, the charm of his genius and the beauty of his style—observing that with a marvellous power of discriminating delicate differences of sentiment, he could match the shades by words "in the choice of which he is often so brilliantly accurate that they gleam upon the paper with the radiance of jewels." "It was, perhaps, in penance for this article," says Sir Charles Dilke, "though she did not repent its doctrine, that, after Pater's death, she bound the copy of his *Renaissance,* which he had presented to her, more beautifully than any other volume in her collection, and reverently placed within it a portrait of the author."[1] As a matter of fact, Mrs. Pattison had no need to do penance for her article. Most critics of Pater—we may say, indeed, all other critics, have assumed that Pater had a wide and deep knowledge of art and the other subjects which he discussed; but the evidence that we have been able to collect does not warrant this assumption. The truth is that Pater, who was of an indolent nature, never would take the trouble to go to the root of things.[2] We have heard it stated, by an authority on these subjects, that his knowledge of art, and even of Greek art, was not very much more profound than Goldsmith's of zoology; but this is an exaggeration. Whatever his limitations, however, he certainly had Goldsmith's wonderful gift—the gift inherent in genius of gilding whatever knowledge he possessed—no matter how insignificant; and that being the case, his very moderate equipment need not trouble us. In those days there were probably a hundred scholars who knew considerably more about art than the author of the *Renaissance,* but there was only one Pater. But Pater was something far higher than a mere scholar. He was a creator.[3]

[1] *The Book of the Spiritual Life,* by the late Lady Dilke, with a memoir of the Author by the Rt. Hon. Sir Charles Dilke, M.P., 1905.
[2] See also Chapter XXXIX.
[3] And he drew his inspiration chiefly from chats with friends and the contemplation of pictures.

CHAPTER XXIX

1874

JOWETT'S SALUTARY WHIP

BIBLIOGRAPHY:

26. Wordsworth. *Fortnightly Review*, 1874, April.
27. Measure for Measure. *Fortnightly Review*, 1874, Nov.

That coveted office the Proctorship, which is the prize of each college in its turn, had in the year 1874 become the gift of Brasenose;[1] and Pater felt virtually certain that upon him the choice would fall—though probably a more unsuitable man for Proctor could not have been found in the whole University. The strengthless, timid, irresolute Pater, followed at a respectful distance by a pair of "bull-dogs" and doing the policeman's work of the University, would have been a sight both remarkable and rememberable. Still, the office had been as good as promised him, and he had already calculated the amount of pleasure in continental travel that the extra remuneration would afford. There was, however, one man to be reckoned with—namely, Benjamin Jowett. With Pater's *Renaissance,* indeed, Jowett had been distinctly displeased, and he summed up its author in a particularly stinging epigram which it is not necessary to repeat. Had Pater, however, put upon his tongue the bridle that had accompanied his pen, then he would have saved himself much mortification. But it was not so, and when his tongue ran away with him, as it had a habit of doing, his best friends felt uncomfortable. Several of them cooled

108. Jowett's Salutary Whip.

---

[1] Brasenose would get it about every ten years.

towards him, while others, though they continued the friendship, were troubled with an uneasy feeling (justifiable or not) that he was doing a certain amount of harm in Oxford. Jowett's animosity towards Pater was increased by the construction which he put upon the rumours to which the inconsequent talk just alluded to gave origin—matters being brought to a head by a casual observation made by a common friend to Jowett; and having said this—that is, just sufficient to justify Jowett—we have said enough. Henceforward Jowett's attitude towards Pater may be discovered in the Hookerian enquiry: "How should the brightness of wisdom shine where the windows of the soul are of very set purpose closed?" The consequence was that Pater lost the coveted post (worth from £300 to £350 for the year) which fell instead to Mr. John Wordsworth.[1]

Mr. A. C. Benson, when touching upon this incident (page 55 of his *Walter Pater*), says: "One feels that Jowett, with his talents for frank remonstrance, had better have employed direct rather than indirect methods." We can only say—with the whole of the facts before us—that Jowett's conduct throughout this affair was that of a Christian and a gentleman. He could not possibly have dealt with the matter more skilfully or more delicately.

Commemoration Week commenced that year on June 14th. On Tuesday, the 16th, there was held in St. John's College Gardens, under the auspices of the Royal Oxford Horticultural Society, a grand Flower Show—six large tents being filled with flowers. The grass was brown and dry, but the sky was overcast, and there blew an icy north wind, which not even the girdle of fine trees, which is so marked a feature of these grounds, could considerably mitigate. It shrivelled up the more delicate of the ornamental plants, it bit, as

[1] In the *Oxford Undergraduates' Journal* Ingram Bywater is referred to as Junior Proctor as late as 5th March 1874, and John Wordsworth as Junior Proctor 27th April 1874.

MR. EDMUND GOSSE.

Photo by Elliott and Fry.

with pincers, the thinly-protected arms of the ladies who had come in their smartest and flimsiest summer dresses. However, they got what pleasure they could out of pelargonium, rose, peach and melon. The measured music of the band mingled with the hum of voices. In the midst of these floods of colour and sound moved one man to whom nothing seemed to appeal. It was Walter Pater, who passed restlessly hither and thither with lowered head. Presently he saw sauntering a few yards off the friend to whom reference has been made. "Do you know," he whispered, as he passed him, "that you lost me three hundred pounds?"

The gain, however, to Pater was infinitely more than the loss—for, henceforth, he kept a very wayward tongue under stricter control; and one may allocate to this period the beginning of the nobler Pater.

During the next few years Pater's principal friends seem to have been Mr. Edmund Gosse, Mr. C. Lawrence Shadwell, the Rev. Mandell Creighton, afterwards Bishop of London, and the Rev. Lewis Campbell. To Mr. Gosse, who was only twenty-three when he made Pater's acquaintance, we have already alluded. He had already written a number of poems; and Pater, who, many years after, reviewed the volume entitled *On Viol and Flute*,[1] singled out for special praise the breezy lines commencing:

109. Mr. Edmund Gosse, Mandell Creighton, and The Rev Lewis Campbell.

"Now, giant-like, the tall young ploughmen go."

Creighton was at this time Fellow and Tutor of Merton College, Oxford. Between him and Pater there was not a great deal in common, though they could talk together freely on art and Ecclesiastical History.

Once at a dinner at Bradmore Road, at which Creighton and Bonamy Price were present, the conversation ran upon ecclesiastical topics, and Pater, who now frequently attended ornate services, both

[1] *Guardian*, 27th October 1890.

Anglican and Roman Catholic, launched out dreamily and "with spring flower sickliness," on the beauty of the Reserved Sacrament in the Roman Church. "It was as though," Creighton used to add when telling the tale, "he was describing a house in which lay a dead friend." Bonamy Price, a Protestant to the backbone, made a sarcastic comment, with the result that the discussion became so heated that Creighton was obliged to insist on their retiring to the drawing-room.

Professor Campbell, who by his *Life of Benjamin Jowett,* written in collaboration with E. Abbot, has made all lovers of literature his debtor, was nine years Pater's senior, and had been Tutor of Queen's College from 1856 to 1858. Mr. Campbell recalls the fact that Pater's pupils, though worshippers of their tutor, were not very successful at the schools. He says: "His conversation and his philosophy magnetised them, but the knowledge obtained in that way was not, as his pupils were to discover 'the sort that paid'; 'and one pupil, in particular,' who wrote gushingly, got 'only a Fourth.'"

Other friends of this period were the Rev. C. H. O. Daniel (now Provost of Worcester College), Mr. Thomas Herbert Warren (now President of Magdalen), Dr. Appleton, editor of *The Academy,* Mr. Basil Champneys, the architect, Thomas Hill Green and Mr. and Mrs. Humphry Ward. Concerning the last three, by reason of the *Robert Elsmere* link, it will be necessary to add a few words. Born in 1836, Green had entered Balliol in 1855, and five years after became a Fellow. Indolent[1] and dreamy, he nevertheless, speedily attained a reputation that must have been flattering to him, and it was considered a privilege to attend his lectures on History and Philosophy. While Matthew Arnold was by a grateful country employed in inspecting little girls'

110. T. H. Green, Mr. and Mrs. Humphry Ward.

---

[1] According to his biography.

needlework, Green was trying to knock Aristotle into the dullards of Balliol. "You should be more genial and facile with your pupils," remarked a friend. "I can't," replied Green, "I don't like the breed." Pater, who was wiser, recognised the fact that all men must spend a portion of their life with dullards, and agreed with his master, Flaubert, who said, "One should live like a middle-class man and think like a demi-god." In 1871 Green married the brilliant and accomplished Miss Charlotte Symonds,[1] who used playfully to style him "Sir Bors"—the knight "who spake so low and sadly at our board." [2]

Mr. Humphry Ward, who was educated at Brasenose, and became Fellow of that College in 1869, had for several years been intimate with Pater, and the friendship lasted till Pater's death. Mr. Ward, as all the books tell us, was the laureate of Brasenose, having addressed a set of pathetic verses to the famous Brasenose ale. This notable brew had for years inspired poet and poetaster; but when Brasenose had produced Mr. Humphry Ward she "could," as Dryden would have said, "no farther go." It would be agreeable to quote stanzas from some of the other sets of verses, but we must restrict ourselves to the following from Mr. Ward's:

> Oh! Brasenose ale, I shrewdly guess,
> You, if you have a conscience,
> To many blunders must confess,
> To many hours of idleness
> And failures in Responsions. [3]

In 1872 Mr. Ward was married to Miss Mary Augusta Arnold—whose name is now a household word; but of Mrs. Humphry Ward, as a novelist, the only remark we need make is that two of the characters in her *Robert Elsmere,* namely, Mr. Grey and Edward Langham, are generally held to be built up mainly and respectively from T. H. Green and Walter Pater.

[1] Sister of J. A. Symonds.
[2] Tennyson: The Holy Grail.
[3] See *Brasenose College,* by John Buchan.

END OF VOLUME I.